POCKET
CHEF

Low Fat

igloobooks

igloobooks

Published in 2016
by Igloo Books Ltd
Cottage Farm
Sywell
NN6 0BJ
www.igloobooks.com

Food photography and recipe development:
© Stockfood, The Food Media Agency
Cover image © Iain Bagwell / Getty Images

HUN001 0216
2 4 6 8 10 9 7 5 3 1
ISBN 978-1-78557-535-8

Cover designed by Nicholas Gage
Interiors designed by Charles Wood-Penn
Edited by Caroline Icke

Printed and manufactured in China

Contents

Snacks
and
Treats

Omelette Pizza

SERVES **1**

PREPARATION TIME **5 MINUTES**

COOKING TIME **5 MINUTES**

INGREDIENTS

2 large eggs
1 tbsp tomato passata
a pinch of dried oregano
1 medium tomato, sliced
a handful of rocket (arugula)
a few Parmesan shavings
salt and black pepper

METHOD

1. Lightly beat the eggs together to break up the yolks and season with salt and pepper.

2. Heat a small non-stick frying pan, then pour in the egg.

3. Cook until it starts to set round the outside, then carefully flip it over and spread the cooked side with the passata and sprinkle it with oregano.

4. Cook for 2 more minutes or until the underside is cooked through, then slide the omelette onto a plate and top with the tomato, rocket and Parmesan.

TOP TIP
Sprinkle a few capers over the top for a tangy finish.

Smoked Salmon and Apple Roulades

SERVES 2

PREPARATION TIME **15 MINUTES**

INGREDIENTS

1 green apple, cored
1 lemon, juiced
100 g / 3 ½ oz / ⅔ cup cold smoked salmon

METHOD

1. Cut the apple into very thin matchsticks with a mandolin, then place in a bowl with the lemon juice and toss to coat.

2. Separate the smoked salmon slices and lay them out in a rectangle on a piece of cling film so that each one just overlaps the other.

3. Drain the apple and lay it in a strip down one edge of the salmon. Using the cling film to help you, carefully roll up the salmon to completely enclose the apple.

4. Cut the roll across into six pieces and skewer with cocktail sticks.

TOP TIP
Add a sprig of watercress to each roulade for extra flavour.

Low-fat Potato Rosti

SERVES 4

PREPARATION TIME 1 HOUR 30 MINUTES

COOKING TIME 45 MINUTES

INGREDIENTS

800 g / 1 lb 12 oz / 4 cups waxy potatoes
2 shallots, thinly sliced
2 tbsp sage leaves, roughly chopped
2 tsp Dijon mustard
2 large egg whites
2 tbsp olive oil
a handful of rocket (arugula)
salt and black pepper

METHOD

1. Cook the unpeeled potatoes in boiling water for 18 minutes or until a skewer slides in easily. Drain well, then leave to cool completely before peeling.

2. Coarsely grate the potatoes. Reserve a little shallot for the garnish and mix the rest into the potato with the sage.

3. Whisk the mustard into the egg white and season with salt and pepper, then stir it into the potatoes. Shape the mixture into twelve flat patties, then chill for 30 minutes.

4. Preheat the oven to 200°C (180°C fan) / 400F / gas 6. Line a baking tray with a non-stick baking mat. Carefully transfer the rostis to the tray and brush the tops with olive oil.

5. Bake the rostis for 25 minutes or until golden brown. Garnish with rocket and the reserved shallot slices.

TOP TIP

These rosti are also delicious made with watercress instead of rocket.

Griddled Courgettes

SERVES 4

PREPARATION TIME 5 MINUTES

COOKING TIME 15 MINUTES

INGREDIENTS

medium courgettes (zucchinis)
lemon, cut into wedges
small bunch of mint, chopped
salt and black pepper

METHOD

1. Top and tail the courgettes, then cut them in half lengthways. Cut each half in half across the middle, then season liberally with salt and pepper.

2. Heat a griddle pan until smoking hot, then cook the courgettes, cut side down, for 8 minutes. Turn the courgettes over and cook on the curved side until tender.

3. Transfer the courgettes to a serving plate, then squeeze over a little lemon juice and sprinkle with mint. Serve with the rest of the lemon wedges.

TOP TIP
Fresh dill makes a great alternative to the mint.

15

Artichoke Hearts with Anchovies and Tomatoes

SERVES 2

PREPARATION TIME 10 MINUTES

COOKING TIME 25 MINUTES

INGREDIENTS

6 frozen artichoke hearts, defrosted
1 clove of garlic, crushed
a pinch of chilli (chili) flakes
3 ripe tomatoes, skinned and chopped
6 salted anchovy fillets, rinsed
6 basil leaves
salt and black pepper

METHOD

1. Preheat the oven to 180°C (160°C fan) / 350F / gas 4.

2. Arrange the artichoke hearts in a single layer in a baking dish.

3. Stir the garlic and chilli flakes into the chopped tomato and season with salt and pepper. Spoon the tomato mixture onto the artichokes then top each one with an anchovy fillet.

4. Bake the artichokes for 25 minutes or until the centres are tender. Garnish with basil and serve immediately.

TOP TIP

For a vegetarian alternative, replace the anchovies with capers.

Vegetable Juice

METHOD

1. Cut the carrot, apple, pepper and tomato into large chunks, then pass through a vegetable juicer with one of the mint sprigs.

2. Stir in the Worcestershire sauce and serve immediately, garnished with the remaining mint sprig.

SERVES 1

PREPARATION TIME 10 MINUTES

INGREDIENTS

2 carrots
1 apple
1 red pepper
1 tomato
2 mint sprigs
a few drops Worcestershire sauce

TOP TIP
Add a 2.5 cm (1 in) piece of ginger to the juicer for a spicy kick.

Tahini Dip

SERVES 6

PREPARATION TIME 10 MINUTES

INGREDIENTS

2 tbsp tahini paste
1 clove of garlic, crushed
a pinch of ground cumin
1 lemon, juiced
225 g / 8 oz / 1 cup fat-free Greek yogurt
225 g / 8 oz / 1 cup fat-free fromage frais
1 tbsp mint leaves, finely chopped
1 tsp sesame seeds
vegetable batons to serve
sea salt and black pepper

METHOD

1. Stir the tahini, garlic and cumin into the lemon juice with a big pinch of salt to dissolve. Stir the mixture into the yogurt and fromage frais with 2 tsp of the mint and taste for seasoning.

2. Spoon the dip into a serving bowl. Dry fry the sesame seeds in a small pan until they turn golden and smell fragrant, then sprinkle them over the dip with the rest of the mint.

3. Serve with vegetable batons for dipping.

TOP TIP
This dip can also be used to dress falafel wraps.

Mixed Vegetable Hummus

SERVES 6

PREPARATION TIME **10 MINUTES**

COOKING TIME **10 MINUTES**

INGREDIENTS

1 carrot, finely chopped
1 celery stick, finely chopped
¼ cauliflower, finely chopped
400 g / 14 oz / 1 ½ cups canned chickpeas
    (garbanzo beans), drained
1 clove of garlic, crushed
1 tbsp tahini paste
1 lemon, juiced
1 tbsp flat leaf parsley, chopped
wholemeal pitta bread, to serve
salt and black pepper

METHOD

1. Bring a saucepan of salted water to the boil, then add the vegetables and cook for 10 minutes or until tender. Drain well, then mix with the chickpeas and mash coarsely with a fork.

2. Stir in the garlic, tahini paste and lemon juice, then season to taste with salt and pepper.

3. Garnish the hummus with parsley and serve with toasted pitta bread.

TOP TIP

Try adding a few drops of sesame oil to enhance the tahini flavour.

Smoked Salmon Blini Omelette

SERVES 1

PREPARATION TIME 5 MINUTES

COOKING TIME 5 MINUTES

INGREDIENTS

2 large eggs
1 tbsp fat-free Greek yogurt
2 slices smoked salmon
1 small shallot, finely chopped
a few sprigs of dill
salt and black pepper

METHOD

1. Lightly beat the eggs together to break up the yolks and season with salt and pepper.

2. Heat a small non-stick frying pan, then pour in the egg.

3. Cook until it starts to set round the outside, then carefully flip it over and cook for 2 more minutes or until the egg is just set in the centre.

4. Slide the omelette onto a plate and leave to cool a little, then spread with the yogurt. Top with the smoked salmon, shallot and dill. Sprinkle with black pepper and serve immediately.

TOP TIP

Try scattering over a few baby capers for a piquant finish.

Steamed Vegetable Rolls

MAKES 6

PREPARATION TIME **15 MINUTES**

COOKING TIME **12 MINUTES**

INGREDIENTS

large cabbage leaves
small carrot, julienned
small courgette (zucchini), julienned
spring onions (scallions), shredded lengthways
2 tbsp fresh root ginger, finely shredded
cloves of garlic, crushed
soy sauce for dipping

METHOD

1. Blanch the cabbage leaves in boiling water for 4 minutes to soften. Drain well, then lay the leaves out on a large chopping board.

2. Mix the carrot, courgette and spring onions with the ginger and garlic, then divide them between the cabbage leaves. Roll each leaf into a parcel, tucking in the sides as you go.

3. Transfer them to a steamer and steam for 8 minutes or until the vegetables are tender but retain a bit of bite. Serve warm with the soy sauce for dipping.

TOP TIP

Dip the rolls in sweet chilli (chili) sauce for a spicy kick.

Poached King Prawns

SERVES 4

PREPARATION TIME 5 MINUTES

COOKING TIME 4 MINUTES

INGREDIENTS

3 tbsp Shaoxing rice wine
1 tbsp light soy sauce
1 tbsp caster (superfine) sugar
4 slices fresh root ginger
24 raw king prawns, peeled with tails left intact
2 spring onions (scallions), thinly sliced
coriander (cilantro) leaves to garnish
black pepper

METHOD

1. Put the rice wine, soy sauce, sugar and ginger in a saucepan with 500 ml / 17 fl. oz / 2 cups of water and bring to a simmer.

2. Add the prawns to the pan, then cover with the lid, turn off the heat and leave to poach gently for 4 minutes.

3. Drain the prawns and divide between four warm bowls, then garnish with black pepper, spring onion and coriander leaves.

TOP TIP
This method can also be used to cook langoustine.

Coconut and Melon Kisses

MAKES 24

PREPARATION TIME **30 MINUTES**

COOKING TIME **10–15 MINUTES**

INGREDIENTS

2 large egg whites
100 g / 3 ½ oz / ½ cup caster (superfine) sugar
250 g / 9 oz / 1 ¼ cups unsweetened
    shredded coconut
1 orange-fleshed melon

METHOD

1. Preheat the oven to 170°C (150°C fan) / 325F / gas 3.

2. Whisk the egg whites to stiff peaks in a very clean bowl, then carefully fold in the sugar and coconut.

3. Spoon the mixture into a 24-hole silicone mini cupcake mould and bake for 10–15 minutes or until they start to turn golden on top.

4. Transfer to a wire rack and leave to cool completely.

5. Use a melon-baller to spoon half-spheres out of the melon, then skewer a piece of melon onto each coconut kiss.

TOP TIP

Mango makes a refreshing and tropical alternative to the melon.

Banana and Kiwi Tray Bake

MAKES 15

PREPARATION TIME 25 MINUTES

COOKING TIME 15–20 MINUTES

INGREDIENTS

3 very ripe bananas
110 g / 4 oz / ⅔ cup soft light brown sugar
2 large eggs
120 ml / 4 fl. oz / ½ cup sunflower oil
225 g / 8 oz / 1 ½ cups wholemeal flour
2 tsp bicarbonate of (baking) soda
2 kiwi fruit, peeled and sliced

METHOD

1. Preheat the oven to 200°C (180°C fan) / 400F / gas 6 and line a 15 cm x 25 cm (6 in x 10 in) baking tin with greaseproof paper.

2. Mash the bananas with a fork, then whisk in the sugar, eggs and oil.

3. Sieve the flour and bicarbonate of soda into the bowl and stir just enough to evenly mix all the ingredients together.

4. Spoon the mixture into the baking tin and level the surface, then transfer the tin to the oven and bake for 15–20 minutes. Test with a wooden toothpick, if it comes out clean, the cake is done.

5. Leave the cake to cool completely in the tin, then turn it out and cut it into 15 squares. Top each with a slice of kiwi fruit.

TOP TIP

Add 1 tsp of ground ginger to the cake mixture for a spicy kick.

Apricot and Banana Flapjacks

MAKES **10**

PREPARATION TIME **5 MINUTES**

COOKING TIME **30 MINUTES**

INGREDIENTS

2 ripe bananas
100 ml / 3 ½ fl. oz / ⅓ cup runny honey
100 g / 3 ½ oz / ½ cup low-fat baking margarine
450 g / 1 lb / 4 ½ cups rolled porridge oats
75 g / 2 ½ oz / ⅓ cup dried apricots, chopped

METHOD

1. Preheat the oven to 190°C (170°C fan) / 375F / gas 5.

2. Put the bananas in a blender with the honey and margarine and blend until smooth. Stir in the oats and apricots, then spoon into a greased baking tin and level the surface.

3. Bake for 30 minutes or until golden brown and cooked through.

4. Cut into ten bars while still warm, but leave to cool completely before removing from the tin.

TOP TIP
Try replacing the dried apricots with dried pears.

Low-fat Brownies with Strawberries

MAKES 9

PREPARATION TIME 25 MINUTES

COOKING TIME 20-25 MINUTES

INGREDIENTS

50 g / 1 ¾ oz / ½ cup unsweetened cocoa powder
50 g / 1 ¾ oz / ½ cup rolled porridge oats
1 tsp baking powder
75 g / 2 ½ oz / ½ cup light brown sugar
175 g / 6 oz / ¾ cup low-fat natural yogurt
50 ml / 1 ¾ fl. oz / ¼ cup skimmed milk
1 large egg
150 g / 5 ½ oz / 1 ¼ cups mixed nuts,
    finely chopped
6 large strawberries, sliced
3 borage flowers

METHOD

1. Preheat the oven to 200°C (180°C fan) / 400F / gas 6 and line a 20 cm (8 in) square baking tin.

2. Put the cocoa, oats, baking powder, sugar, yogurt, milk, egg and nuts in a food processor and blend until smooth and evenly mixed.

3. Spoon the mixture into the baking tin and level the surface, then transfer the tin to the oven and bake for 20–25 minutes. Test with a wooden toothpick, if it comes out clean, the cake is done.

4. Leave the cake to cool completely in the tin, then turn it out and cut it into nine squares. Top each square with a few slices of strawberry and garnish with borage petals

TOP TIP

Add the grated zest of an orange to the brownie mixture for added zing.

Apricot Upside-down Cake

SERVES 8

PREPARATION TIME 20 MINUTES

COOKING TIME 25–35 MINUTES

INGREDIENTS

2 x 420 g cans apricot halves in juice
3 large eggs
100 g / 3 ½ oz / ½ cup caster (superfine) sugar
1 tsp lemon zest
150 g / 5 ½ oz / 1 cup self-raising flour
1 tsp baking powder

METHOD

1. Preheat the oven to 180°C (160°C fan) / 350F / gas 4 and line a 25 cm (10 in) square cake tin with greaseproof paper. Drain the apricots, reserving the juice, and arrange them in the bottom of the tin.

2. Separate the eggs and put the yolks in one bowl and the whites in another. Use an electric whisk to whip the egg whites until they form stiff peaks, then set aside.

3. Use the whisk to beat the yolks with the caster sugar and lemon zest for 4 minutes or until very thick and creamy, then whisk in 6 tbsp of the reserved apricot juice.

4. Sieve over the flour and baking powder, then fold it in carefully with a large metal spoon.

5. Fold in the egg whites, being careful to retain as much air as possible.

6. Scrape the cake mixture into the cake tin and level the surface with a palette knife.

7. Bake the cake for 25–35 minutes or until a skewer inserted in the middle comes out clean. Leave the cake to cool in the tin for 15 minutes, then turn out onto a plate and serve warm or at room temperature.

TOP TIP
This recipe is also delicious made with plums in place of the apricots.

Apple and Date Cake

SERVES 8

PREPARATION TIME 15 MINUTES

COOKING TIME 55 MINUTES

INGREDIENTS

225 g / 8 oz / 1 ½ cups self-raising flour
100 g / 3 ½ oz / ½ cup low-fat baking margarine
100 g / 3 ½ oz / ½ cup caster (superfine) sugar
1 large egg
75 ml / 2 ½ fl. oz / 1/3 cup skimmed milk
2 apples, peeled and chopped
75 g / 2 ½ oz / 1 cup stoned dates, chopped
icing (confectioners') sugar for dusting

METHOD

1. Preheat the oven to 180°C (160°C fan) / 350F / gas 4 and line a loaf tin with greaseproof paper.

2. Sieve the flour into a mixing bowl and rub in the margarine until it resembles fine breadcrumbs, then stir in the sugar.

3. Lightly beat the egg with the milk and stir it into the dry ingredients with the fruit until just combined, then scrape the mixture into the tin.

4. Bake the cake for 55 minutes, or until a skewer inserted into the centre comes out clean.

5. Transfer the cake to a wire rack and leave to cool completely, then sprinkle with icing sugar.

TOP TIP
This cake can be made with dried figs in place of the dates.

Fatless Sponge Financiers

MAKES **12**

PREPARATION TIME **20 MINUTES**

COOKING TIME **8–10 MINUTES**

INGREDIENTS

2 large eggs, separated
85 g / 3 oz / ⅓ cup caster (superfine) sugar
50 g / 1 ¾ oz / ⅓ cup self-raising flour
icing (confectioners') sugar to dust

METHOD

1. Preheat the oven to 180°C (160°C fan) / 355F / gas 4 and oil a 12-hole silicone financier mould.

2. Whisk the egg yolks and caster sugar together for 4 minutes or until pale and thick, then fold in the flour.

3. Whip the egg whites to stiff peaks in a very clean bowl, then fold them into the cake mixture in two stages.

4. Spoon the mixture into the mould, being careful to retain as many air bubbles as possible, and bake for 8–10 minutes or until golden brown and springy to the touch.

5. Leave to cool for 10 minutes, then turn out of the mould and sprinkle with icing sugar.

TOP TIP
Add the finely grated zest of a lemon to the mixture for extra zing.

Apple Soufflé Omelette

SERVES 1–2

PREPARATION TIME 20 MINUTES

COOKING TIME 20 MINUTES

INGREDIENTS

1 dessert apple, peeled, cored and chopped
100 ml / 3 ½ fl. oz / ½ cup unsweetened
    apple juice
½ tsp ground ginger
4 large eggs
1 tsp lemon zest
2 tbsp runny honey
1 tsp lemon juice

METHOD

1. Simmer the apple with the apple juice and ground ginger in a small non-stick frying pan for 10 minutes or until the apple pieces are tender. Drain off any excess liquid.

2. Preheat the grill and separate the egg whites and yolks into two bowls. Whisk the yolks, lemon zest and honey with an electric whisk for 4 minutes or until very thick and pale.

3. In a separate bowl, whisk the egg whites with the lemon juice and a pinch of salt until stiff, but not dry. It's important to make sure that the bowl and beaters are clean and completely grease-free.

4. Heat the apples in their frying pan again until sizzling. Fold the egg whites into the egg yolk mixture, then carefully pour it over the apples and smooth the top.

5. Fry without disturbing until the mixture starts to set round the outside, then put the pan under the grill and cook until the top is golden brown and puffy.

6. Slide the omelette onto a plate and serve immediately.

TOP TIP
This recipe is also delicious made with pears instead of apples.

Muesli Biscuits

MAKES 15

PREPARATION TIME 15 MINUTES

COOKING TIME 25 MINUTES

INGREDIENTS

400 g / 14 oz / 4 cups unsweetened muesli

1 large egg, plus 2 egg whites

60 ml / 1 ¾ fl. oz / ¼ cup maple syrup

1 tbsp brown sugar

METHOD

1. Preheat the oven to 160°C (140°C fan) / 325F / gas 3 and line a Swiss roll tin with a non-stick baking mat.

2. Put half the muesli in a food processor and grind to a coarse flour, then mix with the rest of the muesli in a bowl.

3. Beat the egg with the extra whites until frothy, then stir in the maple syrup and brown sugar.

4. Stir the egg mixture into the muesli a little at a time until it reaches the consistency of soft dough.

5. Press the mixture into the Swiss roll tin in a thin, even layer. Transfer the tin to the oven and bake for 25 minutes or until golden brown.

6. Mark the biscuit into squares while it's still warm, then leave to cool completely before turning it out of the tin.

TOP TIP

Serve the biscuits with low-fat frozen yogurt.

47

Iced Clementines

MAKES *8*

PREPARATION TIME *20 MINUTES*

FREEZING TIME *3 HOURS*

INGREDIENTS

12 clementines
1 egg white
2 tbsp icing (confectioners') sugar

METHOD

1. Cut the tops off the clementines and squeeze the juice into a jug. Reserve 8 of the empty skins.

2. Pour the clementine juice into an ice cube tray and freeze until solid.

3. Transfer the frozen cubes to a food processor with the egg white and icing sugar, then process to a smooth sorbet.

4. Spoon the sorbet into the clementine skins and replace the tops, then freeze until firm.

TOP TIP

This recipe works well with tangerines and mandarins, too.

Crêpes with Lemon and Sugar

ERVES 4

REPARATION TIME 5 MINUTES

OOKING TIME 20 MINUTES

NGREDIENTS

50 g / 5 ½ oz / 1 cup plain (all-purpose) flour
large egg
25 ml / 11 ½ fl. oz / 1 ⅓ cups skimmed milk
sprays 1-cal oil spray
lemon, juiced
tbsp caster (superfine) sugar

METHOD

1. Put the oven on a low setting. Sieve the flour into a bowl and make a well in the centre. Break in the egg and pour in the milk, then use a whisk to gradually incorporate all of the flour from round the outside.

2. Put a non-stick frying pan over a medium heat and spray with oil. Add a small ladle of batter and swirl the pan to coat the base. When it starts to dry and curl up at the edges, turn the pancake over with a spatula and cook the other side until golden brown and cooked through.

3. Transfer the pancake to a plate, cover with a clean tea towel and keep warm in the oven. Repeat the process until all the batter has been used, keeping the finished pancakes warm under the tea towel.

4. Drizzle each pancake with a little lemon juice and sprinkle with sugar, then roll them up and serve immediately.

TOP TIP

Try replacing the sugar with a drizzle of runny honey.

Lunches

Fruit and Vegetable Slaw

SERVES 4

PREPARATION TIME 15 MINUTES

INGREDIENTS

1 red apple, cored
1 lemon, juiced
2 oranges
½ white cabbage
1 red pepper, deseeded
1 green pepper, deseeded
50 g / 1 ¾ oz / ½ cup walnut pieces
1 tsp Dijon mustard
100 g / 3 ½ oz / ½ cup fat-free Greek yogurt
salt and black pepper

METHOD

1. Cut the apple into very thin matchsticks wi a mandolin, then put them in a bowl with th lemon juice and toss to coat.

2. Slice the top and bottom off the oranges. Slice away the peel then cut out each individual segment, leaving the white pith behind. Discard the pith.

3. Shred the cabbage and finely slice the peppers with a sharp knife. Drain the apple reserving the lemon juice, then toss the apple with the orange segments, cabbage, peppers and walnuts.

4. Stir the mustard into the yogurt with enough of the reserved lemon juice to mak a pourable dressing. Season to taste with salt and pepper, then stir it into the slaw.

TOP TIP
This slaw tastes great served with barbecued meat.

Citrus-cured Sardines

SERVES 2

PREPARATION TIME 3 HOURS 15 MINUTES

INGREDIENTS

orange
emon, juiced
bsp sea salt
resh sardines, boned and butterflied

METHOD

1. Use a citrus zester to pare the orange zest into thin strips and set aside.

2. Squeeze the orange and mix the juice with the lemon juice and salt, stirring until it dissolves.

3. Lay the sardines in a single layer in a non-metallic dish and pour over the curing liquid. Cover the dish with cling film and leave to cure in the fridge for 3 hours.

4. Remove any excess marinade from the sardines, then roll each one up and secure with a cocktail stick. Sprinkle over the orange zest and serve immediately.

TOP TIP
This method also works well for curing herring or mackerel.

Grilled King Prawns with Mango Sauce

SERVES **4**

PREPARATION TIME **10 MINUTES**

COOKING TIME **4 MINUTES**

INGREDIENTS

1 ripe mango, peeled and stoned
1 lime, juiced
1 tbsp light soy sauce
24 raw king prawns, peeled with tails left intact
coriander (cilantro) leaves to garnish
freshly ground black pepper

METHOD

1. Put the mango, lime juice and soy sauce in liquidizer and blend until smooth. Taste for seasoning and add a little more soy sauce if needed.

2. Cook the prawns under a hot grill for 2 minutes on each side or until they turn completely opaque.

3. Serve the prawns on a pool of mango sauc garnished with coriander leaves and fresh ground black pepper.

TOP TIP
You can also use monkfish in place of the prawns.

Turkey, Brie and Cranberry Rolls

SERVES 2

PREPARATION TIME 5 MINUTES

INGREDIENTS

2 white baps
2 tbsp cranberry sauce
a handful of sprouting seeds
100 g / 3 ½ oz / ⅓ cup ripe light brie, sliced
150 g / 5 ½ oz / ½ cup cooked turkey
   breast, sliced

METHOD

1. Cut the baps in half and spread with cranberry sauce. Sprinkle the sprouting seeds over the lower half of the rolls and top with the brie and turkey.

2. Close the rolls and cut each one in half before serving.

TOP TIP
You can also use redcurrant jelly in place of the cranberry sauce.

Gazpacho Soup

METHOD

1. Put the cucumber, onions, tomatoes, pepper, vinegar and basil in a liquidizer and blend until smooth.

2. Pass the mixture through a sieve and season to taste with salt and pepper.

3. Pour into four bowls and garnish with basil. Serve with toasted baguette.

SERVES 4

PREPARATION TIME **10 MINUTES**

INGREDIENTS

½ cucumber, peeled and diced
2 spring onions (scallions), finely chopped
250 g / 9 oz / 1 cup ripe tomatoes, cubed
1 red pepper, deseeded and diced
2 tbsp sherry vinegar
1 tbsp basil leaves, shredded, plus extra
    to garnish
8 slices baguette, toasted
salt and black pepper

TOP TIP
This soup looks pretty garnished with finely diced cucumber and red pepper.

Chicken and Fennel Salad

SERVES 2

PREPARATION TIME 40 MINUTES

INGREDIENTS

1 fennel bulb
2 tsp caster (superfine) sugar
1 lemon, juiced
2 tbsp fat-free Greek yogurt
3 spring onions (scallions), sliced
150 g / 5 ½ oz / ½ cup roasted chicken
     breast, sliced
½ cos lettuce, chopped
a small piece of Parmesan
sea salt

METHOD

1. Cut off the green tops of the fennel and reserve as a garnish. Use a mandolin to slice the bulb into thin matchsticks.

2. Stir the sugar and a big pinch of salt into the lemon juice, then pour it over the fennel and leave to cure and soften for 30 minutes.

3. Stir the yogurt and spring onions into the fennel, then toss it with the chicken breast and lettuce.

4. Divide between two bowls, then shave over some Parmesan. Garnish with the fennel fronds and serve.

TOP TIP
Add a few chopped anchovies for a delicious tangy flavour.

Beetroot-cured Salmon

SERVES 8

PREPARATION TIME 1 HOUR

CURING TIME 2 DAYS

INGREDIENTS

4 medium beetroot, grated
75 g / 2 ½ oz / ⅓ cup fine sea salt
75 g / 2 ½ oz / ⅓ cup caster (superfine) sugar
1 tbsp lemon zest, finely grated
1 tsp cracked black pepper
3 tbsp fresh dill, chopped
3 tbsp vodka
1 whole salmon fillet
wholemeal toast and dill sprigs to serve

METHOD

1. Mix together the beetroot, salt, sugar, lemon zest, pepper, dill and vodka and scatter half of it over the base of a large baking dish.

2. Put the salmon on top, skin side down, and spread the rest of the curing mixture on top.

3. Cover the surface with cling film and put a wooden board on top to weigh it down. Leave to cure in the fridge for 2 days.

4. When the curing time is up, scrape off the beetroot mixture, rinse the salmon with cold water and pat dry with kitchen roll.

5. Cut it into very thin slices with a sharp knife and serve with wholemeal toast and sprigs of dill.

TOP TIP
The salmon can be replaced with a large rainbow trout.

Griddled Scallops and Melon

SERVES 4

PREPARATION TIME 5 MINUTES

COOKING TIME 15 MINUTES

INGREDIENTS

tbsp caster (superfine) sugar
tbsp fish sauce
lime, juiced
clove of garlic, crushed
red chilli (chili), finely chopped
scallops
melon, cut into 12 wedges
tbsp salted peanuts, chopped
tbsp coriander (cilantro) leaves, chopped

METHOD

1. To make the dressing, stir the caster sugar into the fish sauce and lime juice to dissolve, then stir in the garlic and chilli.

2. Heat a griddle pan until smoking hot, then cook the scallops and melon for 2 minutes on each side or until nicely marked.

3. Transfer the scallops and melon to four warm plates and drizzle with the dressing. Sprinkle with peanuts and coriander and serve immediately.

TOP TIP

Mango makes a tasty sweet and fleshy alternative to the melon.

Lentil Burgers

SERVES 4

PREPARATION TIME 30 MINUTES

COOKING TIME 15 MINUTES

CHILLING TIME 2 HOURS

INGREDIENTS

250 g / 9 oz / 2 cups red lentils
2 spring onions (scallions), finely chopped
2 cloves of garlic, crushed
1 tsp ground cumin
1 tsp ground coriander (cilantro) seeds
100 g / 3 ½ oz / ⅔ cup gram flour
salt and black pepper

To serve
4 granary rolls, split
4 tbsp hummus
a handful of rocket (arugula)
1 courgette (zucchini)
1 carrot
2 spring onions (scallions), chopped

METHOD

1. Cook the lentils in boiling water for 20 minutes or until tender, then drain well

2. Put the lentils in a food processor with the spring onions, garlic, spices and gram flour and pulse until evenly mixed. Season with salt and pepper.

3. Shape the mixture into four burgers, then chill in the fridge for 2 hours.

4. Preheat the oven to 200°C (180°C fan) / 400 / gas 6. Transfer the burgers to a greased baking tray and bake for 15 minutes or until cooked through.

5. To build the burgers, spread the rolls with hummus and lay the burgers inside on a bed of rocket.

6. Use a vegetable peeler to cut the courgette and carrot into ribbons and sprinkle over the spring onions. Season with salt and pepper and serve immediately.

TOP TIP
Try rolling the lentil mixture into 'meatballs' and serve falafel-style in a flatbread.

Lentil and Sweet Potato Soup

SERVES 6

PREPARATION TIME 2 MINUTES

COOKING TIME 1 HOUR

INGREDIENTS

600 g / 14 oz / 3 ¼ cups red lentils
1 small sweet potato, peeled and diced
2 cloves of garlic, crushed
1 tbsp fresh root ginger, finely chopped
2 tsp mild curry powder
1.2 litres / 2 pint / 5 cups vegetable stock
2 tbsp fat-free natural yogurt
flat leaf parsley to garnish
salt and black pepper

METHOD

1. Put the lentils, sweet potato, garlic, ginger, curry powder and vegetable stock in a saucepan and bring to the boil. Turn down the heat and simmer for 30 minutes or until the lentils and potato are completely tender.

2. Transfer the soup to a liquidizer and blend until smooth. Season to taste with salt and pepper.

3. Ladle the soup into warm bowls and top with a spoonful of yogurt and a sprinkle of parsley.

TOP TIP
This soup tastes great made with butternut squash instead of sweet potato.

73

Roasted Fig and Goats' Cheese Salad

SERVES 2

PREPARATION TIME 5 MINUTES

COOKING TIME 5 MINUTES

INGREDIENTS

8 ripe figs, quartered
2 tbsp runny honey
100 g / 3 ½ oz / ½ cup crumbly goats' cheese
50 g / 1 ¾ oz / 1 cup baby spinach leaves
2 slices prosciutto, thinly shredded
2 tbsp basil leaves
½ tsp smoked paprika
salt and pepper

METHOD

1. Preheat the oven to 180°C (160°C fan) / 350F / gas 4.

2. Spread the figs out in a roasting tin and drizzle with honey. Season with salt and pepper, then roast for 5 minutes.

3. Toss the warm figs with the goats' cheese and spinach leaves and divide between two bowls.

4. Scatter over the shredded ham and basil leaves and sprinkle with paprika, then serve immediately.

TOP TIP
Try using quartered ripe peaches in place of the figs.

Salmon Tacos with Mango Salsa

SERVES 4

PREPARATION TIME **10 MINUTES**

INGREDIENTS

- / 1 ¾ oz / 2 cups mixed leaf salad
- rn taco shells
- g / 14 oz / 1 ½ cups tinned salmon
- ne, juiced
- d chilli (chili), finely chopped
- sp half-fat soured cream

the salsa

- ge mango, peeled and stoned
- cumber
- d chilli (chili), finely chopped
- all bunch fresh coriander (cilantro), chopped
- ne, juiced
- salt

METHOD

1. First make the salsa. Cut the mango and cucumber into small cubes and toss with the chilli, coriander and lime juice. Season to taste with salt.

2. Divide the lettuce between the taco shells. Mash the salmon with a fork and stir in the lime juice and chilli.

3. Divide the salmon mixture between the tacos and top with the soured cream, then serve with the mango salsa on the side.

TOP TIP

Try this recipe with tuna instead of the salmon.

Fig and Smoked Ham Salad

SERVES **4**

PREPARATION TIME **10 MINUTES**

INGREDIENTS

8 ripe figs
150 g / 5 ½ oz / ½ cup wafer-thin smoked ham
a handful of baby chard leaves
a small bunch of celery leaves, shredded
1 tbsp runny honey

METHOD

1. Cut the figs into quarters.

2. Divide the ham and salad leaves between four bowls, then arrange with the figs.

3. Drizzle with a little honey and serve immediately.

TOP TIP

This salad is also tasty when fresh, ripe peaches are paired with the ham.

Smoked Salmon and Cream Cheese Bagels

ERVES 4

REPARATION TIME 10 MINUTES

IGREDIENTS

sesame bagels
bsp low-fat soft cheese
slices smoked salmon
red onion, thinly sliced
g / 1 oz / 1 cup rocket (arugula)
courgette (zucchini)
ime, halved
bsp capers in brine, drained

METHOD

1. Slice the bagels in half and spread one side of each with low-fat soft cheese.

2. Lay the smoked salmon on top, then scatter over the sliced red onion and half of the rocket.

3. Use a vegetable peeler to slice the courgette into long ribbons, then roll up the rest of the rocket inside.

4. Squeeze a little lime juice over the courgette rolls and smoked salmon, then position the other bagel halves on top.

5. Serve with the courgette rolls and capers.

TOP TIP

Try combining the cream cheese with a little lemon zest for added zing.

Mushroom Salad

SERVES **2**

PREPARATION TIME **5 MINUTES**

INGREDIENTS

100 g / 3 ½ oz / 1 ⅓ cups button mushrooms, sliced
2 tomatoes, quartered
25 g / 1 oz / 1 cup mixed salad leaves
a few sprigs watercress
2 tbsp sushi seasoning

METHOD

1. Toss the mushrooms, tomatoes, salad leaves and watercress together and divide between two bowls.

2. Dress with the sushi seasoning and serve immediately.

TOP TIP
Liven up the salad with a few drops of soy sauce.

Lettuce Soup

SERVES 6

PREPARATION TIME 5 MINUTES

COOKING TIME 5 MINUTES

INGREDIENTS

2 litres / 2 pint / 5 cups vegetable stock
iceberg lettuce, chopped
carrot, coarsely grated
00 g / 3 ½ oz / 1 ⅓ cups button mushrooms,
    sliced
small bunch of chives, cut into short lengths
alt and black pepper

METHOD

1. Bring the vegetable stock to the boil in a large saucepan, then stir in the lettuce, carrot and mushrooms.

2. Bring back to the boil and simmer for 2 minutes, then season to taste with salt and pepper.

3. Stir in the chives and serve immediately.

TOP TIP
This soup is a refreshing beverage served chilled in the summer.

Beetroot and Courgette Carpaccio

SERVES 4

PREPARATION TIME 45 MINUTES

INGREDIENTS

2 courgettes (zucchinis)
2 shallots, peeled
1 large beetroot
75 ml / 2 ½ fl. oz / ⅓ cup white wine vinegar
75 g / 2 ½ oz / ⅓ cup caster (superfine) sugar
25 g / 1 oz / ¼ cup chunk of Parmesan
2 tbsp flat leaf parsley leaves
sea salt

METHOD

1. Cut the courgettes and shallots into wafer thin slices with a mandolin and transfer to a bowl. Slice the beetroot in the same way and transfer to a separate bowl.

2. Put the vinegar and sugar in a small saucepan with 1 tsp of salt and stir over a low heat to dissolve the sugar. Bring to a simmer, then pour half of it over the courgette and the other half over the beetroot. Leave to cool completely, then drain well.

3. Divide the vegetables equally between four shallow bowls, then use a vegetable peeler to shave over the Parmesan. Scatter over the parsley and serve immediately.

TOP TIP

On special occasions, add a few wafer-thin slices of lean beef fillet.

Red Mullet Salad

SERVES 2

PREPARATION TIME 5 MINUTES

COOKING TIME 5 MINUTES

INGREDIENTS

lemon
tbsp white wine
bay leaf
sprigs of dill
2 small red mullet fillets
0 g / 1 ¾ oz / 2 cups mixed salad leaves
ea salt

METHOD

1. Cut 3 slices of lemon and put them in a saucepan with the wine, bay leaf and dill, then add 500 ml / 17 fl. oz / 2 cups of water and 1 tsp of salt.

2. Bring the pan to a simmer, then add the mullet to the pan. Cover with the lid, turn off the heat and leave to poach gently for 5 minutes.

3. Arrange the salad leaves in two bowls. Drain the mullet and divide between the bowls. Squeeze over the rest of the lemon and serve immediately.

TOP TIP
A few baby capers make a piquant addition.

Grilled Chicken and Melon Salad

SERVES 2

PREPARATION TIME **35 MINUTES**

COOKING TIME **10 MINUTES**

INGREDIENTS

2 tbsp balsamic vinegar
1 tbsp runny honey
1 tsp Dijon mustard
4 small chicken breasts
½ orange-fleshed melon
25 g / 1 oz / 1 cup lamb's lettuce
25 g / 1 oz / 1 cup baby-leaf spinach
salt and pepper

METHOD

1. Stir the balsamic, honey and mustard together, season with salt and pepper, then drizzle it over the chicken and leave to marinate for 30 minutes.

2. Preheat the grill to its highest setting. Grill the chicken for 10 minutes, turning every 2 minutes or until the juices run clear when you insert a skewer into the thickest part.

3. Use a melon baller to scoop the melon into spheres and toss with the lamb's lettuce and spinach.

4. Arrange the chicken on top and spoon over any juices that have collected in the grill tray.

TOP TIP
Try using a mixture of canteloupe and watermelon.

Pan
Bagnat

ERVES 2

REPARATION TIME 5 MINUTES

NGREDIENTS

25 g / 4 ½ oz / ½ cup white tuna in brine, drained
5 g / 1 oz / ¼ cup Niçoise olives, pitted
medium tomato, diced
cm (2 in) cucumber, peeled and diced
hard-boiled egg, peeled and diced
rustic bread rolls

METHOD

1. Flake the tuna with a fork, then mix it with the olives, tomato, cucumber and egg and season to taste with salt and pepper.

2. Cut the rolls in half and stuff them with the tuna mixture. Serve immediately.

TOP TIP

Try adding a handful of chopped, cooked green beans to the filling.

Cheese and Sweetcorn Salad

SERVES 2

PREPARATION TIME 5 MINUTES

INGREDIENTS

1 tbsp runny honey
½ lemon, juiced
150 g / 5 ½ oz / 1 ¼ cups reduced-fat hard cheese
4 tbsp canned sweetcorn
8 cherry tomatoes, halved
25 g / 1 oz / 1 cup lamb's lettuce
salt and black pepper

METHOD

1. Whisk the honey with the lemon juice to make a dressing and season with salt and pepper.

2. Cut the cheese into cubes and toss with the sweetcorn, tomatoes, lettuce and dressing.

3. Divide between two bowls and serve immediately.

TOP TIP
Try replacing the cheese with cubes of cooked turkey breast.

Fig and Parmesan Salad

RVES **4**

EPARATION TIME **10 MINUTES**

GREDIENTS

ipe figs
hallot, thinly sliced into rings
osp runny honey
emon, juiced
g / 1 oz chunk of Parmesan
andful of mint leaves
rigs of rosemary and flowers to garnish
t and pepper

METHOD

1. Cut the figs horizontally across into thick slices and arrange in a ring on four plates. Scatter the shallot rings on top.

2. Stir the honey into the lemon juice, then drizzle it over the figs and season liberally with salt and pepper.

3. Use a vegetable peeler to shave the Parmesan over the top, then garnish with the mint and rosemary.

TOP TIP

This recipe also works well with a mixture of figs and ripe peaches.

Apricot Compote

SERVES 2

PREPARATION TIME **20 MINUTES**

COOKING TIME **5 MINUTES**

INGREDIENTS

100 g / 3 ½ oz / ½ cup caster (superfine) sugar
12 fresh apricots, halved and stoned
freshly grated nutmeg and mint to garnish

METHOD

1. Put the sugar in a saucepan with 200 ml / 7 fl. oz / ¾ cup of water and stir over a low heat until dissolved. When the sugar has dissolved, increase the heat and bring to a simmer.

2. Add the apricots to the pan and simmer for 5 minutes or until tender. Drain the apricots and allow to cool a little, then peel off and discard the skins.

3. Transfer the apricots to a liquidizer and blend to a smooth compote. Taste for sweetness and add a little more sugar if necessary.

4. Spoon the compote into two bowls and sprinkle with nutmeg. Garnish with mint and serve warm or chilled.

TOP TIP
Try using peaches or plums in place of the apricots.

Apple and Goats' Cheese Salad

SERVES 1

PREPARATION TIME **15 MINUTES**

INGREDIENTS

2 green eating apples
½ lemon, juiced
200 g / 7 oz / ¾ cup goats' cheese
1 small romaine lettuce, cut into ribbons
100 g / 3 ½ oz / ½ cup button mushrooms,
      finely sliced
½ pomegranate

METHOD

1. Halve the apples and core, then slice into thin half moons. Tip into a bowl and stir in a little lemon juice to prevent browning.

2. Cut the cheese into thick slices and arrange on a plate with the apple slices and lettuce ribbons. Scatter the sliced mushrooms around the cheese.

3. Holding the pomegranate half skin side up, bash with a wooden spoon to release the seeds, then drizzle over a little more lemon juice. Serve immediately.

TOP TIP
Add chopped walnuts to this salad to create extra crunch.

Chorizo, Mozzarella and Sun-dried Tomato Rolls

SERVES **4**

PREPARATION TIME **35 MINUTES**

COOKING TIME **10 MINUTES**

INGREDIENTS

50 g / 1 ¾ oz / ¼ cup sun-dried tomatoes
4 cheese baton rolls
2 tbsp pesto
2 balls light mozzarella, cubed
50 g / 1 ¾ oz / ¼ cup chorizo, thinly sliced

METHOD

1. Cover the sun-dried tomatoes with boiling water and leave to rehydrate for 30 minutes.

2. Preheat the oven to 180°C (160°C fan) / 350F / gas 4.

3. Cut the rolls in half lengthways and spread one side of each one with pesto.

4. Drain the sun-dried tomatoes and layer them up in the rolls with the mozzarella and chorizo.

5. Wrap each baton in foil and bake for 10 minutes to melt the cheese. Serve warm.

TOP TIP

Try spreading the rolls with tapenade instead of the pesto.

Melon, Ham and Grape Salad

SERVES 4

PREPARATION TIME 5 MINUTES

INGREDIENTS

orange-fleshed melon
150 g / 5 ½ oz / 1 cup green, seedless
    grapes, halved
150 g / 5 ½ oz / 1 ½ cups honey-roast ham, sliced
50 g / 1 ¾ oz / 2 cups lamb's lettuce
1 tbsp white balsamic vinegar
salt and pepper

METHOD

1. Use a melon baller to scoop the melon into spheres, then toss with the grapes, ham and lettuce.

2. Divide between four bowls and dress with the vinegar, then season with salt and pepper.

TOP TIP

Replace the ham with smoked salmon for a luxurious lunch.

105

Pork and Slow-roasted Tomato Rolls

SERVES 4

PREPARATION TIME **10 MINUTES**

COOKING TIME **1 HOUR**

INGREDIENTS

300 g / 10 ½ oz / 2 cups cherry tomatoes
4 wholemeal and sesame bread rolls
1 tbsp grain mustard
200 g / 7 oz / ¼ cup lean roast pork, sliced
a handful of rocket (arugula)

METHOD

1. Preheat the oven to 160°C (140°C fan) / 325F / gas 3.

2. Arrange the cherry tomatoes in a single layer in a roasting tin, then roast for 1 hou? or until the juices have concentrated and t? skins have shrivelled slightly. Leave to co? a little.

3. Cut the rolls in half and spread one side o? each one with mustard. Add a layer of por? before topping with the tomatoes and a fe? rocket leaves.

TOP TIP
Try wafer-thin turkey ham for a classic sandwich combination.

Dinners

Rabbit with Mushrooms and Bacon

SERVES 4

PREPARATION TIME 15 MINUTES

COOKING TIME 40 MINUTES

INGREDIENTS

4 rabbit legs
4 rashers lean back bacon, fat removed
    and chopped
1 onion, finely chopped
150 g / 5 ½ oz / 2 cups button mushrooms, sliced
500 ml / 17 ½ fl. oz / 2 cups chicken stock
2 bay leaves
2 tsp cornflour (cornstarch)
a little freshly grated nutmeg
salt and black pepper

METHOD

1. Preheat the grill to its highest setting.

2. Season the rabbit legs well with salt and
   pepper, then brown them all over under
   the grill.

3. Fry the bacon in a non-stick saucepan
   until it releases some of its fat, then add
   the onions and mushrooms and fry gently
   for 10 minutes or until softened.

4. Pour in the chicken stock and add the bay
   leaves. When the stock starts to simmer,
   add the rabbit legs. Simmer for 30 minutes
   or until the rabbit is tender.

5. Remove the rabbit legs from the pan and
   keep warm. Mix the cornflour with 1 tbsp of
   cold water, then stir it into the pan. Stir over
   a medium heat until the liquid thickens,
   then season to taste with salt, pepper
   and nutmeg.

6. Return the rabbit to the saucepan and heat
   through briefly before serving.

TOP TIP
The rabbit can be replaced with guinea fowl or chicken.

Shepherds' Pie

SERVES 4

PREPARATION TIME 15 MINUTES

COOKING TIME 1 HOUR 10 MINUTES

INGREDIENTS

450 g / 1 lb / 2 cups lean minced lamb
1 small onion, finely chopped
2 cloves of garlic, crushed
1 tbsp thyme leaves
100 g / 3 ½ oz / ¾ cup green beans, chopped
600 ml / 1 pint / 2 ½ cups beef stock
1 tsp cornflour (cornstarch)
salt and black pepper

For the topping

225 g / 8 oz / 1 cup floury potatoes, peeled
    and cubed
115 g / 4 oz / ½ cup cauliflower florets
115 g / 4 oz / ½ cup broccoli florets
1 tbsp skimmed milk
50 g / 1 ¾ oz / ½ cup reduced-fat cheese, grated

METHOD

1. Dry-fry the mince in a large saucepan for 5 minutes or until it starts to brown and release its juices. Add the onion, garlic and thyme and fry for a further 5 minutes, stirring occasionally.

2. Stir in the beans and stock and simmer for 30 minutes.

3. Mix the cornflour with 1 tbsp of cold water, then stir it into the mince. Stir over a medium heat until the liquid thickens, then season with salt and pepper and tip the mixture into a baking dish.

4. While the mince is cooking, boil the potatoes, cauliflower and broccoli in salted water for 10 minutes, or until tender. Drain well, then mash to a smooth purée with the milk. Season to taste with salt and pepper.

5. Preheat the oven to 200°C (180°C fan) / 400F / gas 6. Spoon the vegetable purée on top of the mince and level the surface.

6. Sprinkle over the grated cheese and bake in the oven for 20 minutes or until golden brown.

TOP TIP

Turn this recipe into a cottage pie by using beef mince instead of lamb mince.

113

Stewed Veal with Olives

SERVES 6

PREPARATION TIME 5 MINUTES

COOKING TIME 2 HOURS 45 MINUTES

INGREDIENTS

800 g / 1 lb 12 oz / 4 cups lean veal,
    cut into chunks
1 onion, chopped
3 cloves of garlic, crushed
1 tsp black peppercorns
1 yellow pepper, deseeded and diced
400 g / 14 oz / 2 cups canned tomatoes, chopped
400 ml / 14 fl. oz / 1 ⅔ cups chicken stock
150 g / 5 ½ oz / 1 cup green olives
salt and black pepper

METHOD

1. Mix together all of the ingredients, except
   for the olives, in a large cast iron casserole
   dish and set it over a medium heat.

2. When the liquid starts to simmer, cover the
   dish, turn down the heat and simmer gently
   for 2 hours.

3. Season the sauce to taste with salt and
   pepper, then stir in the olives and simmer
   for a further 30 minutes.

TOP TIP

You can substitute the veal with lean pork or turkey breast.

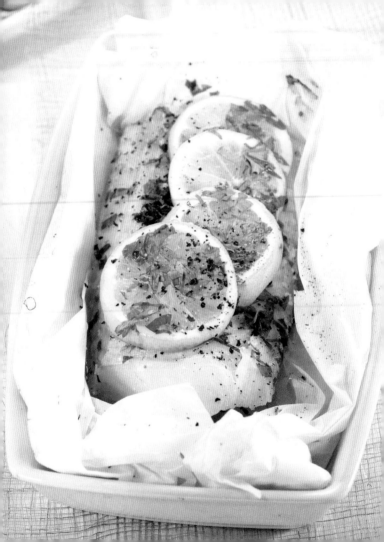

Cod en Papillote

SERVES 2

PREPARATION TIME **10 MINUTES**

COOKING TIME **25 MINUTES**

INGREDIENTS

400 g / 14 oz / 2 cups cod loin
1 clove of garlic, finely chopped
1 small bunch of flat leaf parsley, chopped
1 lemon
salt and black pepper

METHOD

1. Preheat the oven to 200°C (180°C fan) / 400F / gas 6.

2. Line a baking dish with a large sheet of baking parchment and lay the cod in the middle. Sprinkle over the garlic and most of the parsley, then season well with salt and pepper.

3. Cut four slices out of the lemon and lay them on top of the cod, then squeeze over the rest of the lemon and sprinkle with the rest of the parsley.

4. Bring up the sides of the baking parchment to enclose the cod and scrunch the paper together to seal.

5. Transfer the baking dish to the oven and bake for 25 minutes or until the cod just turns opaque in the centre.

TOP TIP
You can use any white fish. Pollock or coley are good sustainable alternatives.

Thai Red Chicken and Vegetable Curry

METHOD

1. Heat the stock and coconut milk together in a saucepan, then stir in the curry paste to dissolve. Add the kaffir lime leaves and bring to a simmer.

2. Stir in the fish sauce and sugar.

3. Add the chicken breast to the pan and poach gently for 5 minutes, then add the vegetables and simmer for 4 minutes.

4. Ladle into four warm bowls and serve garnished with coriander.

SERVES 4

PREPARATION TIME 2 MINUTES

COOKING TIME 12 MINUTES

INGREDIENTS

400 ml / 14 fl. oz / 1 ²/₃ cups chicken stock
100 ml / 3 ½ fl. oz / ½ cup light coconut milk
2 tbsp red Thai curry paste
2 kaffir lime leaves
1 tbsp fish sauce
1 tsp caster (superfine) sugar
150 g / 5 ½ oz / ¾ cup skinless chicken breast, cubed
½ red pepper, deseeded and sliced
75 g / 2 ½ oz ½ cup green beans, halved
2 shallots, sliced
75 g / 2 ½ oz / ½ cup baby corn
1 small courgette (zucchini), halved and sliced
coriander (cilantro) leaves to garnish

TOP TIP

Replace the chicken with roasted aubergine (eggplant) cubes.

Salmon with Courgette Tagliatelle

SERVES 2

PREPARATION TIME 5 MINUTES

COOKING TIME 12 MINUTES

INGREDIENTS

courgettes (zucchinis)
125 g / 4 ½ oz / 2 cups dried tagliatelle
200 g / 7 oz / ¾ cup canned chopped tomatoes
200 g / 7 oz / 2 cups piece salmon fillet, halved
flat leaf parsley to garnish
salt and black pepper

METHOD

1. Preheat the grill to its highest setting.
   Cut the courgettes into long thin julienne
   with a mandolin.

2. Cook the tagliatelle in boiling salted water
   according to the packet instructions or until
   al dente. Add the courgette to the pan and
   warm through for 1 minute, then drain well.

3. While the pasta is cooking, grill the salmon
   for 4 minutes on each side or until only just
   cooked in the centre.

4. Heat the chopped tomatoes until simmering,
   then stir in the tagliatelle and courgette and
   season well with salt and pepper.

5. Serve the salmon with the tagliatelle
   mixture on the side, garnished with parsley.

TOP TIP

The courgette tagliatelle is also delicious served with lean pork chops.

Prawn and Noodle Broth

SERVES 4

PREPARATION TIME 30 MINUTES

COOKING TIME 8 MINUTES

INGREDIENTS

3 tbsp dried black Chinese mushrooms
600 ml / 1 pint / 2 ½ cups fish stock
2 tbsp green Thai curry paste
1 red chilli (chili), sliced
1 tbsp fish sauce
1 tsp caster (superfine) sugar
200 g / 7 oz / 3 ½ cups fresh egg noodles
100 g / 3 ½ oz / ¾ cup sugar snap peas
150 g / 5 ½ oz / ¾ cup raw king prawns, peeled
   with tails left intact

METHOD

1. Cover the mushrooms with boiling water
   and leave to soak for 20 minutes. Drain well
   and cut into thin strips.

2. Heat the stock in a saucepan, then stir in
   the curry paste to dissolve. Stir in the chilli
   fish sauce and sugar, then taste it and adjust
   accordingly.

3. Add the noodles, mushrooms and sugar
   snaps to the pan and simmer for 2 minutes.
   Add the prawns and simmer for 2 more
   minutes, then ladle into four warm bowls
   and serve.

TOP TIP
For a gluten-free alternative, replace the egg noodles with rice noodles.

Lighter Gratin Dauphinoise

SERVES 6

PREPARATION TIME 25 MINUTES

COOKING TIME 30 MINUTES

INGREDIENTS

800 g / 1 lb 12 oz / 4 cups waxy potatoes, peeled
800 ml / 1 pint / 2 ½ cups skimmed milk
4 cloves of garlic, bruised with skin on
1 tbsp thyme leaves
2 bay leaves
4 tbsp half-fat crème fraiche
freshly grated nutmeg for sprinkling
sea salt

METHOD

1. Preheat the oven to 190°C (170°C fan) / 375F / gas 5 and oil a large baking dish.

2. Cut the potatoes into very thin slices with a mandolin.

3. Put the milk in a large saucepan with the garlic, thyme, bay leaves and 1 tsp of salt and bring to a simmer. Add the potatoes and simmer gently for 15 minutes or until the potatoes are tender, but still holding their shape.

4. Drain the potatoes and discard the garlic and bay leaves, then tip them into the baking dish and level the top. Spoon the crème fraiche over the top and sprinkle with nutmeg and freshly ground black pepper.

5. Bake the dauphinoise for 30 minutes or until the top is golden brown and bubbling.

TOP TIP
Serve the dauphinoise with grilled chicken or steamed fish.

Ham and Spinach Lasagne

SERVES 4

PREPARATION TIME 30 MINUTES

COOKING TIME 30 MINUTES

INGREDIENTS

400 g / 14 oz / 2 cups canned tomatoes, chopped
1 onion, finely chopped
2 cloves of garlic, crushed
100 g / 3 ½ oz / 4 cups spinach, washed
300 g / 10 ½ oz / 4 cups fresh lasagne sheets
50 g / 1 ¾ oz / ⅔ cup fresh breadcrumbs
200 g / 7 oz / 1 ½ cups cooked sliced ham,
    chopped
2 tbsp Parmesan, finely grated
salt and pepper

METHOD

1. Put the tomatoes, onion and garlic in a saucepan and simmer for 5 minutes. Season to taste with salt and pepper.

2. Heat a large saucepan, then add the spinach, cover with the lid and allow it to wilt for 2 minutes. Stir well, then turn off the heat.

3. Preheat the oven to 190°C (170°C fan) / 375F / gas 5. Oil a large baking dish and line it with a layer of lasagne sheets. Spread the spinach out on top and season with salt and pepper.

4. Add another layer of lasagne and top with a third of the tomato sauce and a thin layer of breadcrumbs. Top with another layer of lasagne.

5. Stir half of the remaining tomato sauce into the ham and spoon it into the dish, then follow with the final layer of pasta. Spoon over the rest of the tomato sauce, then mix the Parmesan with the rest of the breadcrumbs and scatter it over the top.

6. Transfer the dish to the oven and bake for 30 minutes or until cooked through and golden brown.

TOP TIP

Add a chopped red chilli (chili) to the canned tomatoes for a spicy kick.

Clams Steamed with Sea Salt

SERVES 2

PREPARATION TIME 5 MINUTES

COOKING TIME 5 MINUTES

INGREDIENTS
5 g / 2 ½ oz / ⅓ cup coarse sea salt
sprigs thyme
00 g / 10 ½ oz / 2 cups live clams, scrubbed

METHOD

1. Scatter the salt and thyme over the base of a frying pan, then arrange the clams on top in a single layer.

2. Put a lid on the pan then set it over a high heat and cook for 5 minutes. Check to see if all of the clams have opened – if any are still shut, put the lid back on and cook for 2 more minutes then check again. Serve immediately.

TOP TIP
This recipe also works well with fresh mussels.

Pot-roasted Guinea Fowl

SERVES 2

PREPARATION TIME **15 MINUTES**

COOKING TIME **40 MINUTES**

INGREDIENTS

2 guinea fowl leg quarters
1 leek, halved and sliced
1 carrot, diced
8 baby turnips, peeled
100 g / 3 ½ oz / 2 cups oyster mushrooms,
    torn into strips
2 sprigs fresh sage, plus extra to garnish
200 ml / 7 fl. oz / ¾ cup dry cider
salt and pepper

METHOD

1. Preheat the oven to 180°C (160°C fan) / 350F
   / gas 4 and set the grill to its highest setting.

2. Season the guinea fowl well with salt and
   pepper, then cook the legs skin-side up
   under the grill until nicely browned.

3. Divide the leek, carrots, turnips,
   mushrooms and sage between two
   individual casserole dishes, then lay the
   guinea fowl legs on top.

4. Pour over the cider, then cover the dishes
   and bake them in the oven for 40 minutes.
   Insert a skewer into the thickest part of
   the thigh. If the juice runs clear, the meat
   is cooked.

5. Garnish the dishes with fresh sage and
   serve immediately.

TOP TIP
Try this recipe
with pheasant
when in season.

Spaghetti with Salad Vegetables

METHOD

1. Cook the spaghetti in boiling salted water according to the packet instructions or until al dente.

2. Drain well, then toss with the rest of the ingredients and serve immediately.

SERVES 2

PREPARATION TIME 5 MINUTES

COOKING TIME 12 MINUTES

INGREDIENTS

150 g / 5 ½ oz / 1 ¼ cups dried wholemeal spaghetti
75 g / 2 ½ oz / ²/₃ cup pickled shallots, halved
100 g / 3 ½ oz / ²/₃ cup cherry tomatoes, halved
2 tbsp black olives, pitted and julienned
a handful of rocket (arugula)
2 tbsp balsamic vinegar
sea salt

TOP TIP
This recipe also works well with fresh egg tagliatelle.

Grilled Sea Bass with Peppers and Olives

METHOD

1. Preheat the grill to its highest setting. Grill the peppers for 20 minutes, turning occasionally, until blacked and blistered all over. Transfer the peppers to a mixing bowl and cover tightly with cling film. Leave to steam for 20 minutes.

2. When the peppers are cool enough to handle, peel off the skins and cut each one into four pieces.

3. Season the sea bass with salt and pepper, then cook under the grill for 3 minutes on each side or until just opaque in the centre.

4. Lay the peppers across two warm plates and top with the sea bass. Scatter over the olives and garnish with basil leaves.

SERVES 2

PREPARATION TIME 45 MINUTES

COOKING TIME 6 MINUTES

INGREDIENTS

2 red peppers
2 sea bass fillets
50 g / 1 ¾ oz / ⅓ cup mixed olives
basil leaves to garnish
salt and pepper

TOP TIP

Try using bream or snapper in place of the bass.

Poached Cod with Herbs

METHOD

1. Put all of the ingredients in a large cast iron casserole dish with 1 tsp of sea salt and add enough boiling water to just cover the cod.

2. Bring the pan to a gentle simmer, then cover it with a lid, turn off the heat and leave to gently poach for 15 minutes.

3. Discard the water and herbs and serve the cod with the potatoes and cassava.

SERVES 2

PREPARATION TIME 5 MINUTES

COOKING TIME 15 MINUTES

INGREDIENTS

400 g / 14 oz / 2 cups piece of cod loin
cooked new potatoes, halved
cassava root, peeled and thinly sliced
bay leaves
sprigs of thyme
sprigs of rosemary
sprig of lavender
lemon verbena leaves
salt and pepper

TOP TIP

If you can't find cassava, use thinly sliced celeriac instead.

Roast Guinea Fowl with Asparagus

SERVES 4

PREPARATION TIME **15 MINUTES**

COOKING TIME **30 MINUTES**

INGREDIENTS

4 guinea fowl supremes
225 g / 8 oz / 1 cup white asparagus spears,
    trimmed
225 g / 8 oz / 1 cup green asparagus spears,
    trimmed
1 lemon, juiced and zest finely grated
1 tbsp runny honey
1 tbsp tarragon, finely chopped
150 g / 5 ½ oz / ¾ cup cold-smoked or cured
    haddock loin
salad leaves to serve
salt and black pepper

METHOD

1. Preheat the oven to 180°C (160°C fan)
   / 350F / gas 4.

2. Season the guinea fowl supremes well
   with salt and pepper, then roast them for
   30 minutes or until the juices run clear when
   you pierce the thickest part with a skewer.

3. Meanwhile, steam the asparagus for
   6 minutes or until tender.

4. Mix the lemon juice and zest with the honey
   and tarragon to make a dressing.

5. Cut the haddock into thick slices with a
   sharp knife.

6. Serve the guinea fowl with the steamed
   asparagus on the side. Drizzle over the
   lemon dressing and top each plate with a
   few slices of smoked haddock. Garnish with
   salad leaves.

TOP TIP

Replace the asparagus with purple sprouting broccoli when it's not in season.

Chicken Colombo

SERVES 4

PREPARATION TIME **1 HOUR 15 MINUTES**

COOKING TIME **30 MINUTES**

INGREDIENTS

skinless chicken thighs, cut into chunks
butternut squash, peeled and cut into chunks
aubergine (eggplant), cubed
spring onions (scallions), chopped
cloves of garlic, finely chopped
cm (¾ in) piece ginger, finely chopped
few sprigs of thyme
tbsp Colombo seasoning or mild curry powder
00 ml / 14 fl. oz / 1 ⅔ cups chicken stock
00 ml / 7 fl. oz / ¾ cup light coconut milk
lime, juiced

METHOD

1. Mix the chicken, squash, aubergine, spring onions, garlic, ginger and thyme together in a large saucepan. Sprinkle over the Colombo seasoning and leave to marinate for 1 hour.

2. Pour in the stock and coconut milk then bring to the boil. Cover the pan with a lid, reduce the heat to its lowest setting and simmer gently for 30 minutes or until the chicken is cooked and the squash is tender.

3. Stir in the lime juice and season to taste with salt and pepper.

TOP TIP

For a vegetarian alternative, replace the chicken with cubes of paneer cheese.

141

Chilli Con Carne

SERVES 4

PREPARATION TIME 20 MINUTES

COOKING TIME 2 HOURS 10 MINUTES

INGREDIENTS

2 tbsp vegetable oil
500 g / 1 lb / 2 cups stewing beef, diced
1 onion, peeled and chopped
2 cloves garlic, finely chopped
1 tsp paprika
1 tsp ground cumin
1 tsp cinnamon
½–1 tsp Cayenne pepper
1 x 400 g can kidney beans
1 x 400 g can chopped tomatoes
300 ml / 10 fl. oz / 1 ¼ cups beef stock
salt and black pepper
1 lime, juiced
sour cream, to serve
rice, to serve

METHOD

1. Heat the oil in a large casserole dish and cook the beef until browned. Remove with a slotted spoon and set aside.

2. Add the onion and garlic and fry for 5 minutes until golden.

3. Add the spices and mix well, then pour over the kidney beans, tomatoes and stock. Return the beef to the dish and bring to the boil, then reduce the heat.

4. Simmer over a low heat for at least 2 hours, stirring occasionally, until the chilli has thickened and reduced.

5. When the meat is falling apart, stir and season to taste.

6. Serve with a squeeze of lime juice, sour cream and rice.

TOP TIP
Serve with plain yogurt for a healthier dip.

Orzo Pasta with Rocket and Parmesan

METHOD

1. Cook the orzo in a large pan of boiling salted water according to the packet instructions or until al dente.

2. Drain well, then stir in the rocket and pesto. Season to taste with salt and pepper.

3. Divide the pasta between two bowls and scatter over the Parmesan shavings.

SERVES 2

PREPARATION TIME 5 MINUTES

COOKING TIME 10 MINUTES

INGREDIENTS

200 g / 7 oz / 1 cup dried orzo pasta
50 g / 1 ¾ oz / 1 cup rocket (arugula), chopped
4 tbsp pesto
2 tbsp Parmesan shavings
salt and black pepper

TOP TIP
For a gluten-free alternative, use basmati rice instead of the orzo pasta.

Fettuccine with Roasted Peppers

SERVES 2

PREPARATION TIME 45 MINUTES

COOKING TIME 12 MINUTES

INGREDIENTS

1 red pepper
1 orange pepper
1 yellow pepper
1 green pepper
150 g / 5 ½ oz / ¾ cup dried fettuccine pasta
25 g / 1 oz feta cheese, crumbled
basil leaves to garnish
sea salt and black pepper

METHOD

1. Preheat the grill to its highest setting. Grill the peppers for 20 minutes, turning occasionally, until blacked and blistered all over. Transfer the peppers to a mixing bowl and cover tightly with cling film. Leave to steam for 20 minutes.

2. When the peppers are cool enough to handle, peel off the skins and tear them into strips removing the seeds and core, and set to one side. Pass the contents of the mixing bowl through a sieve to collect the cooking juices produced by the peppers.

3. Cook the fettuccine in boiling salted water according to the packet instructions or until al dente. Drain well then toss with a little of the pepper cooking liquor to moisten.

4. Stir in the peppers, feta and basil leaves and serve immediately.

TOP TIP
Add a finely chopped red chilli (chili) for a spicy kick.

Pork and Vegetable Kebabs

SERVES 4

PREPARATION TIME **30 MINUTES**

COOKING TIME **10 MINUTES**

INGREDIENTS

preserved lemon
450 g / 1 lb / 2 cups lean pork, cubed
8 cherry tomatoes
green pepper, deseeded and cut into chunks
yellow pepper, deseeded and cut into chunks
bay leaves
salt and black pepper

METHOD

1. Prepare a barbecue or preheat the grill to its highest setting and soak eight wooden skewers in cold water for 20 minutes.

2. Cut the preserved lemon into quarters, then scrape out and discard the flesh. Cut each rind quarter into four pieces.

3. Thread the pork, cherry tomatoes, peppers, bay leaves and preserved lemon rind onto the skewers.

4. Cook the kebabs on the barbecue or under the grill for 10 minutes, turning occasionally, until cooked through.

TOP TIP
You can also use chicken in place of the pork.

Baked Red Peppers

SERVES 2

PREPARATION TIME 25 MINUTES

COOKING TIME 45 MINUTES

INGREDIENTS

6 red peppers
1 tbsp balsamic vinegar
2 spring onions (scallions), finely chopped

METHOD

1. Preheat the oven to 220°C (200°C fan) / 425F / gas 7.

2. Arrange the peppers in a single layer in a roasting tin and roast for 45 minutes, turning occasionally.

3. Transfer the peppers to a mixing bowl and cover with cling film then set aside for 15 minutes.

4. When the peppers are just cool enough to handle, peel off and discard the skins.

5. Divide the peppers between two bowls and drizzle with balsamic vinegar. Sprinkle with spring onions and season liberally with salt and pepper. Serve warm or at room temperature.

TOP TIP

Dress the peppers with soy sauce and sesame oil for an Asian alternative.

Asian Grilled Sea Bream

SERVES 4

PREPARATION TIME 25 MINUTES

COOKING TIME 4 MINUTES

INGREDIENTS

½ tsp Chinese five-spice powder

1 tbsp light soy sauce

4 sea bream fillets

200 g / 7 oz / 1 ½ cups sugar snap peas

1 cucumber

4 radishes, thinly sliced

1 tbsp sesame seeds

Salt and black pepper

For the fruit salad

2 small bananas, sliced

2 blood oranges, segmented

1 red chilli (chili), thinly sliced

2 tbsp coriander (cilantro) leaves

METHOD

1. Stir the five-spice into the soy sauce, then brush it over the bream fillets and leave to marinate for 10 minutes.

2. Meanwhile, blanch the sugar snaps in boiling water for 3 minutes, then plunge into cold water and drain well. Peel the cucumber, then cut it in half lengthways and scrape out the seeds. Slice it thinly on the diagonal and toss it with the sugar snaps, radishes and sesame seeds.

3. To make the fruit salad, combine all of the ingredients and divide between four bowls.

4. Preheat the grill to its highest setting. Grill the bream for 2 minutes on each side or until just cooked in the centre.

5. Spoon the vegetables onto four plates and top with the bream fillets and serve the fruit salads on the side.

TOP TIP

The fruit salad makes a great accompaniment to spicy pork chops too.

Asparagus and Mushroom Risotto

SERVES 2

PREPARATION TIME 5 MINUTES

COOKING TIME 30 MINUTES

INGREDIENTS

1 litre / 1 pint 15 fl. oz / 4 cups good quality vegetable stock
4 spring onions (scallions), finely chopped
2 cloves of garlic, crushed
1 lemon, zest finely pared
150 g / 5 ½ oz / ¾ cup risotto rice
100 g / 3 ½ oz / ⅔ cup asparagus spears, cut into short lengths
4 flat cap mushrooms, sliced
4 tbsp low-fat soft cheese
salt and black pepper

METHOD

1. Heat the stock in a saucepan with the spring onions, garlic and lemon zest. When it starts to simmer, tip the rice into a wide saucepan and heat it gently for 2 minutes to warm it through.

2. Add 2 ladles of the hot stock to the rice, then stir in the asparagus and mushrooms. Cook, stirring occasionally, until most of the stock has been absorbed, before adding the next 2 ladles.

3. Continue in this way until all the stock has been used and the rice is just tender, which should take about 15–20 minutes.

4. Stir in the low-fat soft cheese, then cover the pan, turn off the heat and rest for 4 minutes. Uncover the pan and season well with salt and pepper, then spoon into warm bowls.

TOP TIP

Replace the asparagus with sugar snap peas or green beans when it's not in season.

Chicken Kebabs with Potato Salad

SERVES 4

PREPARATION TIME **2 HOURS 10 MINUTES**

COOKING TIME **30 MINUTES**

INGREDIENTS

3 tbsp sun-dried tomato paste

2 tbsp balsamic vinegar

450 g / 1 lb / 2 cups skinless chicken breast, cubed

300 g / 10 ½ / 1 ½ cups oz waxy potatoes

3 tbsp low-fat natural yogurt

1 tbsp lemon juice

1 tsp runny honey

1 tsp Dijon mustard

50 g / 1 ¾ oz / 2 cups salad leaves

chives to garnish

METHOD

1. Mix the tomato paste with the balsamic vinegar, then rub it into the chicken until evenly coated. Leave to marinate for 2 hours.

2. Boil the potatoes whole in their skins for 20 minutes or until a skewer will slide in easily all the way through. Drain well and leave to cool, then cut into thick slices.

3. Prepare a barbecue or preheat the grill to its highest setting and soak eight wooden skewers in cold water for 20 minutes.

4. Thread the chicken onto the skewers then grill or barbecue for 10 minutes, turning occasionally, until cooked through.

5. To make the dressing, mix the yogurt with the lemon juice, honey and mustard and season to taste with salt and pepper.

6. Divide the salad leaves and potato slices between four plates and drizzle with the dressing. Top with the chicken kebabs and garnish with chives.

TOP TIP

For a vegetarian alternative, use halloumi in place of the chicken.

Thai Green Chicken Curry

SERVES 4

PREPARATION TIME 5 MINUTES

COOKING TIME 12 MINUTES

INGREDIENTS

400 ml / 14 fl. oz / 1 ⅔ cups chicken stock
100 ml / 3 ½ fl. oz / ½ cup light coconut milk
2 tbsp Thai green curry paste
2 kaffir lime leaves
1 tbsp fish sauce
1 tsp caster (superfine) sugar
150 g / 5 ½ oz / ¾ cup skinless chicken breast,
     sliced
3 boiled new potatoes, sliced
½ red pepper, deseeded and sliced
6 spring onions (scallions), cut into short lengths
6 cherry tomatoes, halved
purple basil to garnish

METHOD

1. Heat the stock and coconut milk together in a saucepan, then stir in the curry paste to dissolve. Add the kaffir lime leaves and bring to a simmer.

2. Stir in the fish sauce and sugar, then taste it and adjust the levels.

3. Add the chicken breast to the pan and poach gently for 6 minutes, then add the potatoes, red pepper, spring onions and cherry tomatoes and warm through for 4 minutes.

4. Ladle into four warm bowls and serve garnished with purple basil.

TOP TIP

For a vegetarian alternative, replace the chicken with cubes of tofu.

Vegetable Tart

SERVES 6

PREPARATION TIME **2 HOURS 30 MINUTES**

COOKING TIME **25 MINUTES**

INGREDIENTS

- 400 g / 14 oz / 1 ½ cups canned chickpeas (garbanzo beans), drained
- 1 clove of garlic, crushed
- 1 tbsp tahini paste
- 1 lemon, juiced
- 6 asparagus spears
- 1 red onion, sliced
- 1 courgette (zucchini), sliced
- ½ red pepper, deseeded and sliced
- 100 g / 3 ½ oz / ¾ cup preserved artichokes in brine, drained and sliced
- 6 button mushrooms, sliced
- salt and pepper

For the tart case

- 400 g / 14 oz / 2 ⅔ cups strong white bread flour, plus extra for dusting
- ½ tsp easy-blend dried yeast
- 2 tsp caster (superfine) sugar
- 1 tsp fine sea salt

METHOD

1. First make the tart case. Mix together the flour, yeast, sugar and salt then stir in 150 ml / 5 fl. oz / ⅔ cup of warm water. Knead the dough on a lightly oiled surface for 10 minutes or until smooth and elastic.

2. Leave the dough to rest covered with oiled cling film for 1–2 hours until doubled in size. Preheat the oven to 220°C (200°C fan) / 425F / gas 7 and grease a large, non-stick tart case.

3. Knead the dough for 2 more minutes, then roll it out and transfer it to the tart case. Bake the tart case for 10 minutes.

4. Meanwhile, reserve 2 tbsp of chickpeas for the top of the tart and put the rest in a liquidizer with the garlic, tahini paste and lemon juice. Blend until smooth, adding a little water if necessary. Season to taste with salt and pepper.

5. Spoon the hummus into the tart case and arrange the vegetables and reserved chickpeas on top. Return the tart to the oven and bake for 15 minutes or until the vegetables are tender and the tart case is cooked through underneath.

TOP TIP

The bread base makes a great alternative to pastry for any sweet or savoury tart.

Cheese and Sun-dried Tomato Rice Salad

SERVES 4

PREPARATION TIME 40 MINUTES

COOKING TIME 20 MINUTES

INGREDIENTS

50 g / 1 ¾ oz / ¼ cup sun-dried tomatoes
200 g / 7 oz / 1 cup long-grain rice
1 tbsp runny honey
½ lemon, juiced
150 g / 5 ½ oz / 1 ¼ cups reduced-fat hard cheese
2 tbsp chives, chopped
salt and pepper

METHOD

1. Cover the sun-dried tomatoes with boiling water and leave to rehydrate for 30 minutes.

2. Meanwhile, put the rice in a saucepan and add enough water to cover it by 1 cm (½ in).

3. Bring the pan to the boil then cover and turn down the heat to its lowest setting.

4. Cook for 10 minutes then turn off the heat and leave to stand, without lifting the lid, for 10 minutes.

5. Whisk the honey with the lemon juice to make a dressing and season with salt and pepper.

6. When the rice is ready, stir in the dressing and leave to cool a little.

7. Cut the cheese and sun-dried tomatoes into small chunks, then stir them through the salad with the chives. Serve warm or chilled.

TOP TIP
Spice up the salad with a sprinkle of ground cumin.

Desserts

Summer Fruit Meringues

SERVES *8*

PREPARATION TIME **1 HOUR**

COOKING TIME **35 MINUTES**

INGREDIENTS

4 large egg whites
110 g / 4 oz / 1 cup caster (superfine) sugar
300 g / 10 ½ oz / 2 cups mixed summer fruit
2 tbsp runny honey
8 scoops fat-free frozen yogurt
mint leaves to garnish

METHOD

1. Preheat the oven to 140°C (120°C fan) / 275F / gas 1 and oil and line a large baking tray with greaseproof paper.

2. Whisk the egg whites until stiff, then gradually whisk in half the sugar until the mixture is very shiny. Fold in the remaining sugar then spoon the mixture into eight nest shapes on the prepared baking tray.

3. Transfer the tray to the oven and bake for 35 minutes or until the meringues are crisp. Leave to cool completely.

4. While the meringues are cooling, blend half of the summer fruit to a purée with the honey in a liquidizer, then sieve the mixture to remove any seeds.

5. When you're ready to serve, top each meringue nest with a scoop of frozen yogurt and drizzle with the sauce. Scatter over the rest of the summer fruit and garnish with mint leaves.

TOP TIP
Try adding a few drops of rose water to the meringues.

Poached Tomato with Mint Granita

SERVES 4

PREPARATION TIME **10 MINUTES**

COOKING TIME **2 HOURS**

FREEZING TIME **2 HOURS**

INGREDIENTS

1 mint teabag

50 g / 1 ¾ oz / ¼ cup caster (superfine) sugar

1 lemon, juiced

1 tbsp mint leaves, finely chopped

for the tomatoes

150 ml / 5 ½ fl. oz / ²/₃ cup dry white wine

4 large tomatoes

100 g / 3 ½ oz / ²/₃ cup cherry tomatoes

1 tbsp balsamic vinegar

1 tsp red chilli (chili), finely chopped

4 mint sprigs for garnish

salt and black pepper

METHOD

1. Make up the teabag with 250 ml / 9 fl. oz /
   1 cup of boiling water and leave to steep for
   5 minutes. Remove and discard the teabag
   and stir in the sugar. Leave to cool completely.

2. Stir the lemon juice and mint leaves into the
   tea, then transfer to a shallow plastic
   container and put on the lid.

3. Freeze for 2 hours or until almost firm,
   then scrape the mixture into icy grains with
   a fork. Return to the freezer.

4. While the granita is freezing, put the wine in
   a saucepan with 200 ml / 7 fl. oz / ¾ cup of
   water and bring to the boil. Add the large
   tomatoes, then reduce the heat and poach
   gently for 10 minutes or until tender. Drain
   the tomatoes and peel and discard the skins.
   Leave to cool completely.

5. Finely chop the cherry tomatoes and mix
   with the balsamic vinegar, chilli and a pinch
   of salt and pepper. Leave to marinate while
   the tomatoes are cooling.

6. When you're ready to serve, spoon some of
   the cherry tomatoes onto each tomato and
   top with the mint granita and a sprig of mint
   to garnish.

TOP TIP

Try making the granita
with basil in place of
the mint.

DESSERTS

Low-fat Coconut Tart

MAKES **12 SQUARES**

PREPARATION TIME **30 MINUTES**

COOKING TIME **30 MINUTES**

INGREDIENTS

225 g / 8 oz / 1 ½ cups plain (all-purpose) flour
½ tsp baking powder
2 tbsp light brown sugar
50 ml / 1 ¾ fl. oz / ¼ cup sunflower oil
200 g / 7 oz / ⅔ cup raspberry jam (jelly)
2 large egg whites
100 g / 3 ½ oz / ½ cup caster (superfine) sugar
250 g / 9 oz / 1 ¼ cups unsweetened,
    shredded coconut
icing (confectioners') sugar for dusting

METHOD

1. Preheat the oven to 200°C (180°C fan)
   / 400F / gas 6.

2. Stir the flour, baking powder and brown
   sugar together in a bowl. Whisk the oil with
   4 tbsp of cold water until emulsified, then
   drizzle it over the flour. Bring the mixture
   together into a pliable dough, adding a little
   more water if necessary.

3. Roll out the pastry on a floured surface
   and use it to line a greased Swiss roll tin.
   Spread the jam on top.

4. Whisk the egg whites to stiff peaks in a very
   clean bowl, then fold in the caster sugar
   and coconut.

5. Spoon the mixture into a piping bag fitted
   with a large star nozzle and pipe it over the
   surface in an even layer.

6. Bake the tart for 30 minutes or until
   the pastry is cooked underneath and the
   coconut topping is golden brown. Leave to
   cool completely then cut it into 12 squares
   and dust with icing sugar.

TOP TIP
Try replacing the raspberry jam with a generous spread lemon curd.

Waffles

SERVES 6

PREPARATION TIME **10 MINUTES**

COOKING TIME **25 MINUTES**

INGREDIENTS

250 g / 9 oz / 1 ⅔ cups plain (all-purpose) flour

2 tsp baking powder

1 large egg, plus 2 egg whites

300 ml / 10 ½ fl. oz / 1 ¼ cups skimmed milk

100 ml / 3 ½ fl. oz / ½ cup maple syrup

METHOD

1. Put the oven on a low setting and heat a non-stick electric waffle-maker.

2. Mix the flour and baking powder in a bowl and make a well in the centre.

3. Add the eggs and pour in the milk, then use a whisk to gradually incorporate all of the flour from round the outside.

4. Spoon some of the batter into the waffle-maker and close the lid. Cook for 4 minutes or according to the manufacturer's instructions until golden brown. Repeat until all the batter has been used, keeping the finished batches warm in the oven.

5. Drizzle the waffles with maple syrup and serve immediately.

TOP TIP

Serve the waffles with fat-free thick Greek yogurt.

Forest Fruits Sorbet

SERVES 4

PREPARATION TIME 15 MINUTES

FREEZING TIME 2 HOURS 30 MINUTES

INGREDIENTS

400 g / 14 oz / 2 ⅔ cups blueberries and
    raspberries
50 g / 1 ¾ oz / ½ cup icing (confectioners') sugar
1 egg white, lightly beaten
4 light digestive biscuits

METHOD

1. Reserve 100 g / 3 ½ oz / ⅔ cup of the fruit
   and put the rest in the freezer for 2 hours.

2. Transfer the frozen fruit to a food processor
   with the icing sugar and blend until smooth.
   Add the egg white and blend again, then
   scrape the mixture into a plastic tub and
   freeze for 30 minutes.

3. Divide the rest of the berries between
   four glasses and top with scoops of the
   sorbet. Serve immediately with the
   digestive biscuits.

TOP TIP
You can use this method to make strawberry sorbet.

Fruity Jellies

SERVES **4**

PREPARATION TIME **5 MINUTES**

COOKING TIME **5 MINUTES**

SETTING TIME **1–2 HOURS**

INGREDIENTS

500 ml / 1 pint / 2 ½ cups tropical fruit juice
3 g / ¼ oz / ⅓ cup agar agar
2 kiwi fruit, peeled and cubed
8 strawberries, hulled and quartered
shredded mint to garnish

METHOD

1. Heat the fruit juice with the agar agar in a small saucepan until it starts to boil, then turn the heat down and simmer for 5 minutes.

2. Divide the fruit between four glasses, then pour over the agar agar mixture and leave to set.

3. The enzymes in kiwi fruit stop jellies made with gelatin from setting. Agar jellies set at a higher temperature and can therefore be served at room temperature or chilled.

4. Sprinkle with shredded mint before serving.

TOP TIP

Agar agar can be used to set papaya, which is also incompatible with gelatin.

DESSERTS

Pear and Blueberry Verrines

SERVES 4

PREPARATION TIME 10 MINUTES

INGREDIENTS

8 pink sponge fingers
4 tbsp crème de cassis
2 ripe pears, peeled, cored and diced
200 g / 7 oz / 1 ⅓ cups blueberries
225 g / 8 oz / 1 cup fat-free blueberry yogurt

METHOD

1. Crumble the sponge fingers into four glasses and drizzle over the crème de cassis.

2. Top with the fruit, saving a few blueberries for decoration.

3. Spoon the yogurt over the fruit and scatter over the remaining blueberries.

TOP TIP
Try swapping the pears for peaches and the blueberries for raspberries.

Summer Berry Meringue Pudding

SERVES 4

PREPARATION TIME **15 MINUTES**

COOKING TIME **15 MINUTES**

INGREDIENTS

large egg whites
10 g / 4 oz / 1 cup caster (superfine) sugar
00 g / 14 oz / 2 ⅔ cups mixed summer berries

METHOD

1. Preheat the oven to 200°C (180°C fan) / 390F / gas 6.

2. Whisk the egg whites until stiff, then gradually whisk in half the sugar until the mixture is very shiny. Fold in the remaining sugar with a large metal spoon.

3. Tip the berries into a baking dish and spread them out into an even layer. Top with the meringue and swirl it into waves with the back of the spoon.

4. Bake the pudding for 15 minutes or until the meringue is golden brown and set on top.

TOP TIP

Add a floral essence to the meringue with a few drops of rose water.

Raspberry and Almond Rice Puddings

SERVES 6

PREPARATION TIME **15 MINUTES**

COOKING TIME **1 HOUR 30 MINUTES**

COOLING TIME **1 HOUR**

INGREDIENTS

110 g / 4 oz / ½ cup short-grain rice
75 g / 2 ½ oz / ¼ cup runny honey
1.2 litres / 2 pints / 4 ½ cups almond milk
250 g / 9 oz / 1 ⅔ cups raspberries
25 g / 1 oz / ⅓ cup flaked (slivered) almonds

METHOD

1. Preheat the oven to 140°C (120°C fan) / 275F / gas 1.

2. Stir the rice and honey into the almond milk in a baking dish, then cover and bake for 1 hour 30 minutes. Leave to cool.

3. Discard the skin on top of the pudding. Crush half of the raspberries with a fork, then stir the purée into the rice with the whole berries, reserving a few for decoration.

4. Divide the rice pudding between six glasses and sprinkle the almonds and reserved raspberries over the top.

TOP TIP
You can also make the rice pudding with oat milk.

Foamy Lemon Jellies

SERVES 4

PREPARATION TIME **15 MINUTES**

SETTING TIME **2–3 HOURS**

INGREDIENTS

5 sheets leaf gelatin
600 ml / 1 pint / 2 ½ cups traditional still
    lemonade
2 large egg whites
lemon zest to garnish

METHOD

1. Soak the gelatin in a small bowl of cold water for 10 minutes.

2. Heat 200 ml / 7 fl. oz / ¾ cup of the lemonade in a small saucepan until it starts to simmer, then turn off the heat. Squeeze any excess liquid out of the softened gelatin then whisk it into the hot lemonade liquid to dissolve.

3. Stir the hot gelatin mixture into the rest of the cold lemonade, then pour half of it into four glasses. Transfer the glasses to the fridge and leave to chill and set for 2 hours.

4. Allow the rest of the gelatin mixture to cool to room temperature. When it just starts to gel around the edges, whisk the egg whites with an electric whisk in a clean bowl until they reach stiff peaks.

5. Whisk the gelatin mixture with the electric whisk until it looks foamy, then fold in the egg white. Spoon the mixture on top of the lemon jellies and return to the fridge until completely set. Garnish with lemon zest before serving.

TOP TIP

This recipe can be made with pink grapefruit juice in place of the lemonade.

Almond Jelly

SERVES **4**

PREPARATION TIME **15 MINUTES**

SETTING TIME **2–3 HOURS**

INGREDIENTS

4 sheets leaf gelatin
600 ml / 1 pint / 2 ½ cups almond milk
125 g / 4 ¼ oz / ½ cup caster (superfine) sugar
a few drops almond essence
8 almonds

METHOD

1. Soak the gelatin in a small bowl of cold water for 10 minutes.

2. Heat 200 ml / 7 fl. oz / ¾ cup of the almond milk with the sugar in a small saucepan until it starts to simmer, then turn off the heat. Squeeze any excess liquid out of the softened gelatin then whisk it into the hot liquid to dissolve.

3. Stir the hot gelatin mixture into the rest of the cold almond milk with the almond essence, then pour it into four individual jelly moulds.

4. Transfer the moulds carefully to the fridge and leave to chill and set for 2–3 hours.

5. When you are ready to serve, dip the outside of each mould briefly in a bowl of hot water, making sure no water gets into the jelly. Give it a shake to loosen, then turn them out onto four plates and garnish with almonds.

TOP TIP
Add a floral essence to the jelly with a few drops of orange flower water.

Baked Egg Custard with Peaches

SERVES 4

PREPARATION TIME 20 MINUTES

COOKING TIME 45 MINUTES

INGREDIENTS

1 x 420 g / 15 oz can peach slices in juice, drained
500 ml / 17 ½ fl. oz / 2 cups skimmed milk
2 large eggs, plus 1 egg white
50 g / 1 ¾ oz / ¼ cup caster (superfine) sugar
½ tsp vanilla extract

METHOD

1. Preheat the oven to 160°C (140°C fan) / 325F / gas 3.

2. Divide the peach slices between four ramekin dishes. Heat the milk in a saucepan until hot but not boiling.

3. Meanwhile, stir the eggs, egg white and sugar together with the vanilla extract. When the milk is ready, incorporate it into the egg mixture in a thin stream, whisking all the time.

4. Pass the mixture through a fine sieve and divide it between the ramekins. Set the ramekins in a large roasting in and pour enough boiling water around them to come half way up the sides.

5. Transfer the tin to the oven and bake for 45 minutes or until the custards are just set in the centre and the tops are golden brown. Serve warm or chilled.

TOP TIP

These custards also taste great made with apricots in place of the peaches.

DESSERTS

Peach Melba Verrines

SERVES 4

PREPARATION TIME 15 MINUTES

INGREDIENTS

100 g / 3 ½ oz / ⅔ cup raspberries
2 tbsp runny honey
4 ripe peaches, peeled and stoned
1 vanilla pod
225 g / 8 oz / 1 cup fat-free natural fromage frais
225 g / 8 oz / 1 cup fat-free natural yogurt
50 g / 1 ¾ oz / ½ cup icing (confectioners')
    sugar, sieved
2 tbsp toasted flaked (slivered) almonds

METHOD

1. Press the raspberries through a sieve and discard the seeds. Stir the honey into the raspberry pulp to make a thick sauce.

2. Cut the peaches into small cubes and divide half of them between four glasses.

3. Cut the vanilla pod in half lengthways and scrape out the seeds, then stir them into the fromage frais and yogurt with the icing sugar.

4. Spoon half of the yogurt mixture into the glasses, then top with the rest of the peaches.

5. Spoon over the rest of the yogurt and drizzle with raspberry sauce. Garnish with flaked almonds.

TOP TIP

These verrines are also delicious made with mango in place of the peaches.

Strawberry Verrines

METHOD

1. Purée half of the strawberry slices with 2 tbsp of the honey in a liquidizer to make a smooth sauce.

2. Crumble the sponge fingers into four glasses and drizzle over the strawberry sauce, then top with the rest of the strawberry slices.

3. Stir the rest of the honey into the yogurt and spoon it over the strawberries, then garnish the verrines with mint.

SERVES 4

PREPARATION TIME 15 MINUTES

INGREDIENTS

200 g / 7 oz / 1 1/3 cups strawberries, sliced
4 tbsp runny honey
8 sponge fingers
225 g / 8 oz / 1 cup fat-free natural yogurt
4 mint sprigs

TOP TIP

Add 1 tbsp of crème de cassis to each verrine for an adults-only treat.

Grilled Apricot Skewers

SERVES 4

PREPARATION TIME **25 MINUTES**

COOKING TIME **10 MINUTES**

INGREDIENTS

12 fresh apricots
½ tsp orange flower water
2 tbsp runny honey
1 tbsp demerara sugar

METHOD

1. Prepare a barbecue or preheat the grill to its highest setting and soak four wooden skewers in cold water for 20 minutes.

2. Thread 3 apricots onto each skewer. Stir the orange flower water into the honey, then use a pastry brush to coat the apricots in a thin layer.

3. Cook the apricots under the grill for 10 minutes, turning occasionally, until tender and lightly charred in places.

4. Sprinkle with demerara sugar and serve immediately.

TOP TIP
This method also works well with plums.

Cherry and Almond Zabaglione

SERVES 6

PREPARATION TIME 5 MINUTES

COOKING TIME 10 MINUTES

INGREDIENTS

3 large egg yolks
2 ½ tbsp caster (superfine) sugar
2 ½ tbsp amaretto liqueur
225 g / 8 oz / 1 ½ cups cherries, stoned
2 tbsp toasted flaked (slivered) almonds

METHOD

1. Put a raclette grill on to heat.

2. Set a heatproof bowl over a saucepan of simmering water, making sure the bottom of the bowl doesn't come into contact with the water.

3. Add the egg yolks, sugar and amaretto to the bowl and whisk vigorously until thick and creamy. Take the bowl off of the heat.

4. Spoon the zabaglione into six raclette trays and scatter over the cherries. Cook the zabaglione under the raclette grill for 2–3 minutes until golden brown on top, then scatter over the almonds and serve immediately.

TOP TIP

You can use individual baking dishes instead of a raclette, and toast under a hot grill.

Blackberry, Apple and Meringue Compote

SERVES 6

PREPARATION TIME 20 MINUTES

COOKING TIME 15 MINUTES

INGREDIENTS

2 Bramley apples, peeled, cored and chopped
200 g / 7 oz / 1 ⅓ cups blackberries
50 g / 1 ¾ oz / ¼ cup granulated sugar
4 large egg whites
110g / 4 oz / 1 cup caster (superfine) sugar

METHOD

1. Put the apples, blackberries and granulated sugar in a saucepan with a splash of water. Cover the pan and cook over a medium heat for 10 minutes or until it has broken down into a thick compote, stirring occasionally. Spoon the compote into six glasses.

2. Whisk the egg whites until stiff, then gradually whisk in half the sugar until the mixture is very shiny. Fold in the remaining sugar with a large metal spoon.

3. Spoon the meringue into a piping bag fitted with a large star nozzle and pipe a swirl on top of the compote in each glass.

4. Toast under a hot grill for 3–4 minutes or until the tops are golden brown. Serve immediately.

TOP TIP

Try replacing the apples with pears and the blackberries with blueberries.

Summer Berry Rice Puddings

SERVES 6

PREPARATION TIME 15 MINUTES

COOKING TIME 1 HOUR 30 MINUTES

COOLING TIME 1 HOUR

INGREDIENTS

110 g / 4 oz / ½ cup short-grain rice
75 g / 2 ½ oz / ¼ cup runny honey
1.2 litres / 2 pints / 4 ½ cups skimmed milk
250 g / 9 oz / 1 ⅔ cups mixed summer berries
3 meringue nests, crumbled

METHOD

1. Preheat the oven to 140°C (120°C fan) / 275F / gas 1.

2. Stir the rice and honey into the milk in a baking dish, then cover and bake for 1 hour 30 minutes. Leave to cool completely.

3. Discard the skin on top of the pudding. Crush half of the berries with a fork, then stir the purée into the rice with the whole berries and crumbled meringue.

4. Divide the rice pudding between six bowls and serve immediately.

TOP TIP

This rice pudding is also delicious served hot from the oven.

Apricots with Amaretti Cream

SERVES 4

PREPARATION TIME 2 HOURS 15 MINUTES

COOKING TIME 5 MINUTES

INGREDIENTS

250 ml / 8 fl. oz / 1 cup unsweetened apple juice
300 g / 10 ½ oz / 1 ½ cups dried apricots
225 g / 8 oz / 1 cup fat-free natural fromage frais
2 tbsp icing (confectioners') sugar
2 tbsp amaretto liqueur
8 amaretti biscuits

METHOD

1. Bring the apple juice to the boil, then pour it over the apricots and leave to cool and macerate for 2 hours.

2. Spoon the apricots onto four plates. Mix the fromage frais with the sugar and liqueur and spoon it over the apricots, then crumble over the biscuits.

TOP TIP
This method also works well with prunes.

DESSERTS

Roasted Pineapple

SERVES 4

PREPARATION TIME 10 MINUTES

COOKING TIME 25 MINUTES

INGREDIENTS

1 pineapple, peeled and cored
200 g / 7 oz / ¾ cup caster (superfine) sugar
1 cinnamon stick
4 cardamom pods
1 star anise
1 piece orange peel
4 tbsp fat-free fromage frais
8 amaretti biscuits, crushed
4 scoops fat-free frozen yogurt
caramel shards, mint leaves and plum slices
   to garnish

METHOD

1. Preheat the oven to 200°C (180°C fan)
   / 400F / gas 6 and cut the pineapple into
   even-sized batons.

2. Put the sugar, spices and orange peel in
   a saucepan with 300 ml / 10 fl. oz / 1 ¼ cups
   of water and stir over a medium heat to
   dissolve the sugar.

3. Once the sugar has dissolved, stop stirring
   and let it boil for 10 minutes or until thick
   and syrupy. Strain it into a jug to remove
   the spices.

4. Arrange the pineapple in a roasting tin in
   a single layer and pour over three quarters
   of the spiced syrup. Roast the pineapple for
   15 minutes, turning halfway through.

5. Arrange the pineapple batons, in stacks,
   on four plates. Add a spoonful of crushed
   amaretti to each plate and top with a scoop
   of frozen yogurt.

6. Stir a little of the left over syrup into the
   fromage frais and spoon it around the plate,
   then garnish with caramel shards, mint
   leaves and plum slices.

TOP TIP
Try serving the pineapple with mango sorbet as a low-fat accompaniment.

Demerara Meringues

MAKES 8

PREPARATION TIME 20 MINUTES

FREEZING TIME 1 HOUR

INGREDIENTS

4 large egg whites
110 g / 4 oz / 1 cup caster (superfine) sugar
2 tbsp demerara sugar

METHOD

1. Preheat the oven to 140°C (120°C fan) / 275F / gas 1 and oil and line a large baking tray with greaseproof paper.

2. Whisk the egg whites until stiff, then gradually whisk in half the caster sugar until the mixture is very shiny. Fold in the remaining caster sugar with a large metal spoon, being careful to retain as much air as possible.

3. Spoon the meringue into a piping bag fitted with a large star nozzle and pipe eight swirls onto the baking tray. Sprinkle the tops with demerara sugar, then transfer the tray to the oven and bake for 1 hour.

4. Turn off the oven and leave the meringues to cool slowly inside before serving.

TOP TIP
Add a floral essence to the meringues with a few drops of orange flower water.

DESSERTS

Marinated Cherries

SERVES 4

PREPARATION TIME 1 HOUR

COOKING TIME 30 MINUTES

INGREDIENTS

450 g / 1 lb / 3 cups cherries, stoned
1 tbsp caster (superfine) sugar
3 tbsp orange liqueur
a pinch of ground cloves
1 tbsp mint leaves, finely shredded

METHOD

1. Toss the cherries with the sugar, liqueur and ground cloves and leave to marinate for 1 hour.

2. Warm a frying pan over a medium heat. Add the cherries and sauté for 5 minutes or until the juices thicken and glaze the fruit.

3. Serve immediately, sprinkled with mint.

TOP TIP

This recipe is also delicious made with mirabelle plums.

Kiwi Verrines

SERVES **4**

PREPARATION TIME **15 MINUTES**

INGREDIENTS

6 kiwi fruit, peeled
1 lime, juiced
50 g / 1 ¾ oz / ½ cup icing (confectioners')
    sugar, sieved
450 g / 1 lb / 2 cups fat-free natural fromage frais
4 ginger biscuits

METHOD

1. Cut 4 slices of kiwi fruit and reserve for the garnish, then cut the rest into small cubes and toss with the lime juice.

2. Fold the icing sugar into the fromage frais, then spoon the mixture into a piping bag, fitted with a large star nozzle.

3. Divide half of the kiwi mixture between four glass dishes, then pipe a swirl of fromage frais on top. Spoon over the rest of the kiwi and top the verrines with the rest of the fromage frais.

4. Crumble a ginger biscuit over each verrine and garnish with the reserved kiwi slices. Serve immediately.

TOP TIP

Use papaya in place of the kiwi. Remember to remove the seeds.

Baked Spiced Apples

SERVES 6

PREPARATION TIME **10 MINUTES**

COOKING TIME **25 MINUTES**

INGREDIENTS

6 small eating apples, peeled
2 tbsp butter, softened
2 tbsp brown sugar
½ tsp ground ginger
½ tsp ground cinnamon
1 vanilla pod
1 cinnamon stick
1 orange, zest peeled

METHOD

1. Preheat the oven to 180°C (160°C fan) / 350F / gas 4.

2. Arrange the apples in a baking dish.

3. Beat together the butter, sugar, ginger and cinnamon and spices and spread over the apples, then scatter over the vanilla pod and cinnamon stick.

4. Bake in the oven for 25 minutes or until the apples are soft.

TOP TIP

Try this recipe with pears instead of apples.

Marinated Strawberry and Lemon Verrines

SERVES **4**

PREPARATION TIME **40 MINUTES**

INGREDIENTS

4 tbsp balsamic vinegar
200 g / 7 oz / 1 ⅓ cups strawberries, sliced
1 lemon
50 g / 1 ¾ oz / ½ cup icing (confectioners') sugar
225 g / 8 oz / 1 cup fat-free Greek yogurt
225 g / 8 oz / 1 cup fat-free fromage frais

METHOD

1. Pour the balsamic vinegar over the strawberries and leave to marinate for 30 minutes.

2. Use a citrus-zester to finely pare the lemon rind into strips and reserve for the garnish. Squeeze the lemon and mix the juice with the icing sugar to dissolve, then fold it into the yogurt and fromage frais.

3. Divide the yogurt mixture between four glasses and top with the marinated strawberries. Sprinkle with lemon zest and serve immediately.

TOP TIP

Top the verrines with a scoop of lemon sorbet for added guilt-free indulgence.

Poached Mirabelles

SERVES 4

PREPARATION TIME 5 MINUTES

COOKING TIME 6 MINUTES

COOLING TIME 1 HOUR

INGREDIENTS

500 ml / 16 fl. oz / 2 cups weak black tea
300 g / 10 ½ oz / 2 cups fresh mirabelles
4 tbsp ginger syrup
4 tbsp fat-free fromage frais
4 ginger biscuits, crumbled

METHOD

1. Bring the tea to a simmer in a saucepan, then add the mirabelles and poach gently for 6 minutes. Stir in the ginger syrup and leave to cool completely.

2. Spoon the mirabelles into four glasses with some of the cooking liquor then top with fromage frais and sprinkle over the ginger biscuit crumbs.

TOP TIP
This recipe also works well with small greengages or cherries.

Spiced Green Tea Granita

SERVES 4

PREPARATION TIME 5 MINUTES

COOKING TIME 5 MINUTES

FREEZING TIME 2 HOURS

INGREDIENTS

2 green teabags
5 cm (2 in) fresh root ginger, sliced
3 pieces cassia bark
4 cardamom pods
100 g / 3 ½ oz / ½ cup caster (superfine) sugar
1 lemon, juiced
4 sprigs of mint

METHOD

1. Make up the teabags with 500 ml / 17 fl. oz / 2 cups of boiling water. Add the ginger, cassia and cardamom and leave to infuse for 5 minutes. Remove and discard the teabag and stir in the sugar, then leave to cool completely.

2. Strain out the spices and stir the lemon juice into the tea, then transfer to a shallow plastic container and put on the lid.

3. Freeze for 2 hours or until almost firm then scrape the mixture into icy grains with a fork.

4. Divide the granita between four glasses and serve with mint to garnish.

TOP TIP

Try making this granita with rooibos tea instead of green tea.

INDEX

Peach Melba Verrines, 190
Strawberry Verrines, 192

NOODLES
Prawn and Noodle Broth, 122

NUTS, MIXED
Low-fat Brownies with Strawberries, 36

OATS
Apricot and Banana Flapjacks, 34
Low-fat Brownies with Strawberries, 36

OLIVES
Grilled Sea Bass with Peppers and
    Olives, 134
Pan Bagnat, 92
Spaghetti with Salad Vegetables, 132
Stewed Veal with Olives, 114

ONION
Chilli Con Carne, 142
Ham and Spinach Lasagne, 126
Rabbit with Mushrooms and Bacon, 110
Shepherds' Pie, 112
Stewed Veal with Olives, 114
Vegetable Tart, 160

ORANGE
Asian Grilled Sea Bream, 152
Baked Spiced Apples, 213
Citrus-cured Sardines, 56
Fruit and Vegetable Slaw, 54
Roasted Pineapple, 204

ORANGE FLOWER WATER
Grilled Apricot Skewers, 194

ORANGE LIQUEUR
Marinated Cherries, 208

PAPRIKA
Chilli Con Carne, 142

PASTA
Fettuccine with Roasted Peppers, 146
Ham and Spinach Lasagne, 126
Orzo Pasta with Rocket and
    Parmesan, 144
Salmon with Courgette Tagliatelle, 120
Spaghetti with Salad Vegetables, 132

PEACHES
Baked Egg Custard with Peaches, 188
Peach Melba Verrines, 190

PEANUTS
Griddled Scallops and Melon, 68

PEARS
Pear and Blueberry Verrines, 178

PEPPERS
Baked Red Peppers, 150
Fettuccine with Roasted Peppers, 146

Fruit and Vegetable Slaw, 54
Gazpacho Soup, 62
Grilled Sea Bass with Peppers and
    Olives, 134
Pork and Vegetable Kebabs, 148
Stewed Veal with Olives, 114
Thai Green Chicken Curry, 158
Thai Red Chicken and Vegetable
    Curry, 118
Vegetable Juice, 18
Vegetable Tart, 160

PESTO SAUCE
Chorizo, Mozzarella and Sun-dried
    Tomato Rolls, 102
Orzo Pasta with Rocket and
    Parmesan, 144

PINEAPPLE
Roasted Pineapple, 204

POMEGRANATE
Apple and Goats' Cheese Salad, 101

PORK
Pork and Slow-Roasted Tomato
    Rolls, 106
Pork and Vegetable Kebabs, 148

POTATO
Chicken Kebabs with Potato Salad, 156
Lighter Gratin Dauphinoise, 124
Low-fat Potato Rosti, 12
Poached Cod with Herbs, 136
Shepherds' Pie, 112
Thai Green Chicken Curry, 158

PRAWNS
Grilled King Prawns with Mango
    Sauce, 58
Poached King Prawns, 28
Prawn and Noodle Broth, 122

PROSCIUTTO
Roasted Fig and Goats' Cheese
    Salad, 74

RABBIT
Rabbit with Mushrooms and Bacon, 110

RADISHES
Asian Grilled Sea Bream, 152

RASPBERRIES
Forest Fruits Sorbet, 174
Peach Melba Verrines, 190
Raspberry and Almond Rice
    Puddings, 182

RED MULLET
Red Mullet Salad, 88

RICE
Asparagus and Mushroom Risotto, 154

Cheese and Sun-dried Tomato Rice
    Salad, 162
Raspberry and Almond Rice
    Puddings, 182
Summer Berry Rice Puddings, 200

ROCKET (ARUGULA)
Lentil Burgers, 70
Low-fat Potato Rosti, 12
Omelette Pizza, 8
Orzo Pasta with Rocket and
    Parmesan, 144
Pork and Slow-roasted Tomato
    Rolls, 106
Smoked Salmon and Cream Cheese
    Bagels, 80
Spaghetti with Salad Vegetables, 132

SALMON
Beetroot-cured Salmon, 66
Salmon Tacos with Mango Salsa, 76
Salmon with Courgette Tagliatelle, 120

SALMON, SMOKED
Smoked Salmon and Apple
    Roulades, 10
Smoked Salmon and Cream Cheese
    Bagels, 80
Smoked Salmon Blini Omelette, 24

SARDINES
Citrus-cured Sardines, 56

SCALLOPS
Griddled Scallops and Melon, 68

SEA BASS
Grilled Sea Bass with Peppers and
    Olives, 134

SEA BREAM
Asian Grilled Sea Bream, 152

SESAME SEEDS
Asian Grilled Sea Bream, 152
Tahini Dip, 20

SHALLOTS
Beetroot and Courgette Carpaccio, 86
Fig and Parmesan Salad, 96
Low-fat Potato Rosti, 12
Smoked Salmon Blini Omelette, 24
Spaghetti with Salad Vegetables, 132
Thai Red Chicken and Vegetable
    Curry, 118

SHAOXING RICE WINE
Poached King Prawns, 28

SHERRY VINEGAR
Gazpacho Soup, 62

SMOKED PAPRIKA
Roasted Fig and Goats' Cheese
    Salad, 74